IMPOSSIBLE SALES

The Simplest, Logical, Practical, And Accelerated Sales Guide To Supercharge Your Sales Performance

MIHIR KOLTHARKAR

*This book is dedicated to my Dad,
who watches over me from a different realm.*

Impossible Sales
Copyright © 2020 by Mihir Koltharkar

All rights reserved. No part of this book may be used or reproduced in any manner whatsoever without written permission except in the case of brief quotations embodied in critical articles or reviews.

For information contact:
www.impossiblesales.com
www.mihirkoltharkar.com

First Edition: JAN 2020

Preface

With so many books already in circulation, what makes this sales book different?

This book is one of the most straightforward books on sales that assures you of concrete results. It has the best combination of proven practices, models, and theories, which, when combined and followed, will drastically improve your sales. This book is the distillation of my years of continuous learning of sales psychology and buying motivators in the changing world.

An ultra-luxury real estate multinational company headquartered in Dubai increased its turnover by 31%, amounting to $4.51 Billion in 12 months by updating the 800+ sales professionals with the 'Rainbow Giraffe','Red Snapper' and 'Danger and Dangler' approach to Sales.

A leading Building Materials and Home Improvement company increased its turnover by $1.2 Million in 18 months by implementing the 'CIMTA' approach.

A Ship Repair company managed to save $1 Million in just one month after educating their staff with the help of Negotiation Planner, and strategies explained in this book.

It's not just organizations, an entrepreneur who had started his business of Industrial Equipments and had zero clients, managed to get 11 big clients and 30+ small clients, within 6 months after learning the essential sales techniques and tools shared in this book.

There have been many more success stories, and yours can be one of them too.

The premise of this book is to help you discover the art and science of sales. You will find practical solutions to enhance your sales techniques and boost your sales by following time-tested strategies, create engaging sales pitches, increase your conversion percentage, and gain insights on how to increase profit margins. This book will provide you with the techniques that can help you to overcome sales obstacles and to improve your game plan to meet your deadlines, and exceed your targets.

The CIMTA approach will help you to rethink the pattern of your sales pitch, and to understand the value of variety. This book will guide you on that journey to success as it is for everyone who will do what it takes to become an outstanding sales professional. Sales is a mixture of the logical and emotional process from the beginning to the end. If you follow the steps, tools, methods, and techniques mentioned in this book, you would not only achieve sustainable and profitable sales but also exceed your target expectations! It is a simple, no-nonsense approach to help you sow the knowledge, practice the skills, and reap the benefit of abundant sales.

Remember 'Impossible' is just a word, making it 'IM-Possible' is a positive mental attitude.

Formal sales knowledge is a fragile foundation, and if not upgraded at regular intervals, much of it becomes obsolete every few years. We live in an ever-changing world, and it is at lightning speeds that innovation in technology, business strategies, buying psychology and patterns, and other fields always overwhelm us. Therefore, the need of the hour is to keep pace with them, as much as we can. Since the competition is ever increasing and is fierce, learning sales skills becomes a matter of survival. Your ability to adapt will determine your success in the future.

To benefit from the cutting edge techniques presented in this book, and to add value to your knowledge and experience, get habituated to the new way of thinking. Write down what you feel is most vital for you and list the ways you can apply them in your unique situation. To attain success, follow thoughts with action.

So let's start the journey.

1 Sell Efficiently and Profitably

How to make money for yourself and your organization?

Turnover Is Vanity, Profit Is Sanity

Today, every single business faces an aggressive competing environment, which can be a boon in disguise as it pushes them to innovate and be customer-oriented. Evolving competitive environments

"When dealing with people, remember you are not dealing with creatures of logic, but creatures of emotion."

– Dale Carnegie

drive organizations to focus on getting better every day, to unify, strengthen, and expand their market share. In today's market, any business which focuses on the customer and responds to their needs quicker than the others has the edge over the competition. Evaluating a competitor's strengths, weaknesses, and their response to customers' needs, prepares the business for the challenges of the consumer-oriented market.

In a constantly evolving environment, where the customer dominates, businesses scramble to satisfy their needs. How does this affect the salesperson? Earlier, a salesperson was required to be an excellent persuader and an authority on the features of the product. The combination of these two factors made sales possible because the customers had little or no options, and very little access to information about the product.

Today, the salesperson has to take on multiple roles – a subject matter expert, an advisor, a guide, a friend – to provide maximum value to the customer, making traditional sales methods secondary. The dynamic market environment opens up a plethora of choices for the discerning customer. They are not dependent on just one company to satisfy their wants and needs and can select the option that offers maximum benefits. In other words, the customer feels free to go for the best instead of being compelled to buy what is available.

Imagine a scenario for company ABC which has, previously, enjoyed a monopoly for a particular product and is now seeing a decline in sales figures because of increased competition. This situation makes the top brass at ABC to come up with strategies to halt the downhill trend. They decide to infuse more money into advertising, thereby increasing visibility. How does this scenario alter the salesperson's day to day work? The salesperson is assigned new targets, and there is constant pressure to achieve them. Businesses have to adopt this step to remain profitable despite increased expenditure.

The salespeople are at their wit's end as they have to meet their numbers. The situation takes a downward spiral, and the sales department requests for promotional campaigns, discounts, and anything else that would help to achieve targets, making it even harder for ABC to reach Gross Profit or Net Profit. ABC also has to deal with the increasing number of competitors every passing day. Last but not least, the Product Life Cycle also comes into play.

So how does a salesperson cope with these circumstances? The salesperson his left with four options:

- Work overtime to meet targets
- Find another job
- Continue underperforming and get fired for non-performance
- Upgrade their skill-set to meet new challenges

What happens if the salesperson decides to go with:

The First Option?
When the salesperson puts in more time at work, the work-life balance is affected. The stress, magnified by a never-ending workday, puts the salesperson at risk on the personal front – family, health, and overall wellness is at peril. This cycle continues until the salesperson reaches the stage of

burnout. The salesperson decides that he or she cannot continue this process, and will result in choosing the 2nd or 3rd option.

The Second Option?
On the edge of burnout, the salesperson usually decides to go for the second option. If lucky, he/she takes up a position in a new company. But how does this mitigate the situation? The new organization will have its targets to meet. The first couple of months might seem a bit relaxed as the salesperson is learning the ropes. The targets are given sooner or later, and the salesperson is back on the wheel. So this does not solve the problem as a similar cycle of work continues.

The Third Option?
The third option is one that no employee ever wants to face. It leads not only to unemployment and loss of financial security but also a loss of self-esteem and untold difficulties in the personal and professional areas. Getting a new job after being fired for non-performance is never easy. The salesperson might have to compromise on the work profile or salary, which is not desirable at all. Well, then, what does one do?

The Fourth Option?
The relentless pursuit of knowledge is a SMART solution. Continuous learning ensures that you are more employable and ready to move up the corporate ladder. You are putting effort into learning new skills and develop your skillset, which indicates your initiative and enhances your value to

employers. So you are on your way to ensuring job security. In short, constant learning and up-gradation of skills, reinforces your confidence, and increases your credibility with your employers. You are knowledgeable, competent, and proactive. You can offer solutions to problems, and you are self-motivated. Hence, you are an asset to the company.

The pivotal factor that will decide your future in your workplace will be your capability to adapt to change. A fluid marketplace is one that flourishes on chaos and unpredictability. This constant state of flux requires an ever-increasing passion for learning and the application of what learning within the commercial world. One must be flexible in letting go of the old and welcome the new.

Unlearning would require you to open up your mind and broaden your perspective, to strip away anything that obstructs new knowledge. On this clean slate, you will be able to inscribe in detail, expand your knowledge, and put to practical use the new skills you have acquired. So, if you equip yourself with a passionate learning attitude, everything is within your grasp.

Your Expectations:

We have learned what organizations expect from a salesperson. We have identified customer expectations. Now let's discuss You. What are your expectations as a salesperson? What do you want from yourself?

Some of the things that you may be expecting –

- Stability
- Respect and Status
- Finances
- Incentives
- Increasing Contacts
- Position
- Added Responsibilities
- Leadership
- Perks and Benefits
- Travel
- Helping Others

The factors mentioned above are attainable individually or together. To achieve them, you need to sell more and sell profitably. When such a thing happens, the business makes higher profits and rewards you with better incentives. In short, the company treats you like a star employee. So, where do you start? One of the immediate things that are within your hands is to increase Gross Profit for the organization.

Customers nowadays, be it an individual or an organization, generally ask for a discounted price. Who wouldn't want anything for less? Most salespeople cave in immediately at the sight of approaching business. That's the human psychology at work. If you are pressed for targets, and you see an opportunity to sell, you will be in a hurry to close the sale. In this case, you may tend to give a discount for immediate gain. You may get the business as well, but how does this affect the organization's Gross Profit?

Let's calculate-

Imagine the Unit Price of Product X is $10, and the current Profit is 30%. (Cost Price – $7, Profit – $3) and you decide to give a 10% discount to the customer. If you are averaging sales of 100 Units a month:

Before Discount

\	Before Discount
Selling Price	$10.00
Quantity Sold	100
Turnover	$1000
Unit Cost	$7
Unit Profit	$3
Total Cost	$700
Total Profit	$300

Impossible Sales

After Discount

	After Discount
Selling Price	$9
Quantity Sold	
Turnover	
Unit Cost	$7
Unit Profit	$2
Total Cost	
Total Profit	300

To reach the same profit, we will now calculate the number of units needed to sell. So we divide the Profit by Unit Profit.

$300/$2 = 150

The final comparison looks like this:

	Before	Discount	After
Selling Price	$10.00	**10%**	$9.00
Quantity Sold	100		150
Turnover	$ 1000		$ 1350
Unit Cost	$7		$7
Unit Profit	$3		$2.00
Total Cost	$700		$1,050.00
Total Profit	$300		$300.00

This calculation means to reach to the same Gross Profit we need to sell 50% more Units!

Let us look at a 5% Discount Calculation Comparison.

	Before	Discount	After
Selling Price	$10.00	5%	$9.50
Quantity Sold	100		120
Turnover	$ 1000		$ 1140
Unit Cost	$7		$7
Unit Profit	$3		$2.50
Total Cost	$700		$840.00
Total Profit	$300		$300.00

So for a 5% Discount, we need to sell 20% more units. It is fascinating to see the repercussions of a discount. Most of the salespeople are unaware of this calculation and hence end up giving a discount too quickly. Be very cautious in offering discounts, because when the organization looks at making profits, this plays a significant role. Business practices like discounts and loyalty offer help in clearing stock and also drawing in new customers. Clearance sales are a frequent event nowadays. Discounts also help achieve sales targets in slow business periods. But it is vital to plan these price changes (knowledge of current profit margin, markup, and breakeven point) and compute the best discount price to continue making a profit. Not to forget how crucial it is to ascertain what the competitors are offering and their product pricing. If selling 100 units is a challenge and you want to offer a discount, are you in a position to increase the units sold? Is this challenging in the competitive market? What if you increase the price instead of giving a discount? A price increase – though considered as a challenging and uncomfortable step for businesses can turn out to be a good deal. Some customers do not worry about the price if there is value strengthening. The same can be said for loyal customers because they understand the value of your products and services and the existing relationship which caters to their needs and preferences. They comprehend that value is not a one-time offering, which helps them to accept the price increase, and hence they don't involve themselves in unnecessary negotiations.

You can afford to sell less and maintain the profits, isn't it? But the percentage is different.

Impossible Sales

Let us look at the calculation-

	Before	**Increase**	**After**
Selling Price	$10.00	**10%**	$11.00
Quantity Sold	100		75
Total Sales	1000		825
Unit Cost	$7		$7
Unit Profit	$3		$4.00
Total Cost	$700		$525.00
Total Profit	$300		$300.00

If you increase the Selling Price by 10%, and you sell just 75 units instead of 100, your organization will still make the same gross profit! Isn't this interesting?

When you live by numbers, just the turnover of an organization may not indicate its success; however, it is crucial to look at Gross Profit. The calculations above and the figures mentioned are still not the actual profits. If you give a discount of 10%, and you have to sell 50% more units, there are many factors which need to be taken into consideration while selling the additional units:

1. Storage
2. Transportation
3. Manufacturing
4. Workforce
5. Marketing
6. Damaged Goods & Returns
7. Inventory Management
8. Packing and Distribution
9. Business Hours For Strategy Deployment
10. _____ many more factors.

So the actual profit is going to be less than projected.

From a business perspective, it is essential to revise the prices every year for the following reasons:

- Suppliers and vendors increase their prices
- Overall Inflation
- Increase in the salaries of employees
- Marketing costs to keep up with the competition
- The maintenance cost of assets

The cost price or operating expenses will usually go higher, and if the selling price for your product remains the same, the profit percentage will decrease.

Let's take an example – Most of us have a favorite restaurant that we go to or usually order food from them.

Now ask yourself these questions :

- Do you order/have food ONLY from that restaurant?
- Have you never tried a snack or a meal from any other restaurant?
- Have you ever visited a new restaurant and loved the place and food so much that now it has become your new favorite restaurant?
- Has your social circle expanded? You may get invites to different restaurants, which you can't refuse, for maintaining or building relations?
- If your family member likes another place, would you still order from your favorite restaurant?

Well, as the competition increases, people may try out new products in the market just because of the novelty it offers, or out of obligation, translating to a loss in your business. So you need to anticipate the loss of some customers to your competitors every passing month/year.

Price is usually an issue in the absence of value

It is for these factors that many experts would encourage price revision – rather than decreasing the price of your product, increase it. And support it by increasing the value. Increase your value and show ways that help the customer to save money, time, or enhance the quality of their life.

2 Breaking The Impossible Barrier

How to make it possible?

Minding Matters

Successful sales professionals have the freedom to write their paycheck and decide their earnings. The amount they want to earn and achieve is entirely dependent on them. Many sales professionals make more than the management team. The secret lies in what they do to reach this stage in their life. They are the ones who transform Impossible to I-M-Possible.

"Some men see things as they are and ask why... I dream of things that never were and ask why not?"

– Robert Kennedy

This chapter is for mindset conditioning, and even if some experienced professionals may feel they already have the requisite knowledge, I urge you to stay with the book. Remember, irrespective of the years of experience a pilot has, the plane still needs to be appropriately aligned on the runway before the take-off.

Reality check Many sales professionals have made this domain as a career choice for two reasons:

1. Because of the possibilities of making their mark having realized their persuasive skills
2. They didn't get their desired professional choice, and this was the option that was in front

In either of the situation, they have realized that Sales is the driving force of an organization. Without Sales, no enterprise can survive, and hence they are tasked with a considerable responsibility to chase their steadily increasing targets. Due to the acceptance of online shopping models, many of the small ticket items are purchased online, thus transforming the retail sales scenario. However, the same is not applicable for B2B, or products at a high price, as there might be customization required, or there would be multiple people involved in the decision-making process or many other reasons. Selling high-ticket items can be more demanding and challenging and require different approaches, knowledge, skills, and attitude.

Organizations facing the sword of a highly competitive market, are on a constant quest for recruiting dynamic sales professionals who can support in realizing their ambitious targets. They look for people who can represent their brand in the market and get profitable sales closures while targeting an increase in market share.

Business Owners, Independent Consultants, and Entrepreneurs have to rely on constant sales and strive hard to make their mark.

Anytime a new product or a service idea is born and materialized, some opportunists get inspired and are on their toes to replicate with few or more changes, thus creating competition. The innovator can get hunted, and survival depends on profitable sales.

In Today's World, Is Sales Easy Or Difficult?

It's all in the mind!

The blueprint for success in any business relationship is an understanding of the human mind. There are many triggers that prompt behaviors that eventually lead to success or failure.

What is the fine line that differentiates an achiever from a non-achiever? What conditions steer us towards an attitude of success or laxity? How do successful salespeople meet and exceed their targets? The secret formula for success lies within us. I have come across numerous examples where people have doubted their capabilities or have adopted a lackadaisical attitude towards their profession. In the last two decades, during my sales workshops in multiple countries, I always ask my audience, "In the current scenario, is it possible to double your sales?"

Impossible Sales

Human nature, in all its doubts and capabilities, responds in three ways.

90% of the respondents said – That's impossible! We are not even able to achieve our targets. The market is terrible, and competition is increasing. Doubling sales is impossible unless the organization spends a lot on marketing.

8% of the respondents said – We can try. If we strive for the moon, we will land among stars.

2% of the respondents answered – Definitely yes! Everything is achievable. We just need to figure out the path and get adequate resources.

For those who believe that it is achievable, this belief is intrinsic to self-mastery linked to an interest in enriching not only their knowledge but also multiplying their income manifold.

For those who seek inspiration, it's easily noticeable. The animal world, for instance, is full of examples of sharp learning curves. The birth of a giraffe and it's first moments in this world is an excellent illustration of such a learning opportunity and inspiration. Standing up, the mother giraffe gives birth to her baby, which falls more than 5 feet to the ground. As the baby starts recovering from the fall, it is kicked by the mother until it can stand on its own feet. It is excruciating for the little giraffe, but in the wild, the baby needs to learn to flee from predators. There is not even a moment to waste because agility determines survival. Though the baby giraffe learns the first painful lesson, it does not deter from accomplishing the goal of standing up as fast as possible. The mother ensures that her baby learns to survive in a land filled with lions, hyenas, and other predators, who would love to have the baby as their meal.

A new business or a new product in the market will always have competitors who would be eager predators. Selling quickly, sustainably, and profitably requires learning and adapting. Learning takes effort and practice. Learning can be painful and time-consuming; however, it is essential for business survival.

During my workshop, I ask the participants whether they have met successful salespeople, and if they have, were they curious enough to find out what led them to exceed their goals? The answers range from a majority 'No' to a lukewarm 'Sometimes' and an enthusiastic minority that replies 'Yes' with confidence. Those 'Yes' people have an unusually open mind, an intellect receptive to new tactics and strategies along with focus and discipline. To achieve the seemingly impossible targets, you have to set a new action plan. You have to determine what it is that you are trying to accomplish. A clear goal enables you to monitor progress and gather momentum while pursuing it. You also need a strategy to achieve your sales target, learn the art of consultative selling, and the knowledge to maximize revenue from your existing customers.

What Makes It Possible?

Let us revisit our childhood-those beautiful days when we learned how to walk. Babies can be the best teachers we can have for tenacity. Let us follow a baby girl's journey towards taking her first steps.

Creeping – At first, the baby might get around by combat crawling – pull herself forward with her arms and dragging her legs and belly on the ground. Or she might prefer to scamper along sideways or backward on her bottom to reach a toy. Whichever method the baby uses, she lets you know that she is on the path to learning and autonomy.

Crawling – Once the baby is on her knees crawling around, she might spend a short while rocking back and forth before she determines the way to move forward. She will crawl towards her toys and sit for a moment to take a breather, and then she is off again. Your happy reaction and applause, when she succeeds, will make her enthusiastic towards her goal.

Pulling Up – Your baby now uses her stronger arm muscles to help herself to a standing position, taking advantage of whatever's handy – the sofa, the table, the chair, or your leg.

Cruising – Once your baby is acquainted with the feeling of standing upright, she'll attempt a couple of tentative steps with some support. This stage enables the baby to balance and strengthen her muscles.

Walking – The baby grows in confidence and lets go of her support once in a while. She takes a few tentative steps and sits down if the effort tires her. Your encouragement drives her sense of accomplishment, and soon, she takes her first steps towards you with outstretched arms. She may walk/run too fast or too slow, but your joy knows no boundaries now.

Research shows that it takes almost 1000 hours of practice for a baby to walk alone without help. They need to develop coordination and muscle strength by learning how to sit, rollover, and crawl. Then they must pull themselves up with support (holding on to something) and stand. They will fall many times, but that does not mean they give up after a few tumbles. Each fall is a motivator and brings about renewed confidence. Finally, one day, to the delight of their parents, they stand up and take that first step, and then they walk!

What do we mean when we refer to the tenacity of a toddler? We see that toddlers can adjust themselves to the situation to accelerate learning and foster a mindset that enhances motivation. They look beyond short-term apprehensions to higher-order objectives like walking, thus being ready to take on challenges and obstacles to keep going towards their goals. A fall or injury does not deter them. It might be a momentary setback, but they pull on till they succeed.

Do not forget – that toddler was you.

Going back to our childhood once again, I would like to bring to your attention the time when we just started learning the alphabet. It began with the very act of holding the pencil in those little unsteady hands. We had to try many times to be able to position the pencil correctly, and days went by, just perfecting the process. The letters of the alphabet were unfamiliar; the shapes were a challenge to our shaky hands, and memorizing the alphabet was tough. But we did it.

When we were good with the alphabet and the numbers, we learned how to make sentences and then learned sentence patterns, parts of speech, the tenses, and the importance of synonyms and antonyms. We were elated when we unraveled the mysteries of a dictionary and thesaurus. Each day introduced us to something incredible, and we absorbed everything like a sponge. Today, it's all imprinted in our minds – we barely think twice while drafting emails – as the knowledge is ingrained in our minds. What do these examples illustrate? They enable us to understand the behavior of children as active learners, who plan and develop strategies for memory, comprehension, and problem-solving.

Learning new skills or trying them out may have been difficult and discouraging, but as we have all experienced, it is this struggle that helps us to absorb and retrieve the information later. As a Sales & Negotiation Training Professional, I am always delighted to see the participants in my sessions display an eagerness to travel to unknown destinations on a voyage of discovery. That eagerness comes from a curiosity that requires us to stretch our ability to understand, to be passionate learners, to be discerning observers, and to question our assumptions.

Each one of us has learned through a different life-experiences, and have internalized a set of conscious and unconscious beliefs. Some of us had the privilege of formal education, and the rest of us studied at the *University Of Life*.

Whichever method we have chosen, we have comprehended the universe of knowledge and have realized that there is always more to learn. This awareness helps us scale greater heights when we put to use the knowledge available to us.

When we also have a mentor to guide our actions, excellence is just a few steps away.

Is success in sales any different? Right from childhood, we have been strategists and negotiators. We threw a tantrum if we didn't get what we wanted (candy- most of the time). We sold the idea of going to a picnic with our friends by convincing our parents of the benefits it would bring us and the safety methods that we would adopt in case of an emergency. We negotiated with our parents for the bicycle that we wanted and agreed to score the highest grades in exchange for it. We are born negotiators and efficient salespeople, having learned these techniques through trial and error at a very young age. We were our first teachers.

During adulthood, while attending a party or a function, we took utmost care in dressing for the occasion and wore what the occasion demanded. We were particular about how we presented ourselves because the image we projected was vital to us. We were presenting ourselves as a product. We created images of ourselves that are beautiful and powerful. Our personality, our approachability, and most importantly, our ability to stand out in a crowd makes us attractive to others. Is it surprising then that many love stories and friendships take their first steps during a friend's or relative's wedding?

Our life provides us with many such experiences every day, and if we are keen enough, we can learn by observing them minutely. We will see that most of them are lessons in sales and marketing, which can apply to specific situations. Once you make this a habit, you will see that things are relatively simple, being just a matter of execution and practice. Sales, then, becomes a lifestyle, not a profession. So when you adopt a lifestyle, you will find many positive changes in your personal as well as professional life.

Most sales beginners start their sales journey with flawed thinking that selling is easy. It's easy to find customers who would buy because the product is right, or because of influencing skills. It is easier said than done. As newbies in Sales, they are often influenced by other sales professionals or business people and try to follow what the others do – learning by observation or through guidance. They try to know everything about the product, after all, if the customer would ask anything about the product and they don't know the answer, it could be embarrassing. There are rare few who get the opportunity to learn the art of selling and practice their skills. Products, services, and companies can change in a salesperson's career. However, if the selling skills are known and practiced, then success can always be within grasp.

As a sales newbie, the attitude of learning will carve a path for future glory. Remember the toddler tenacity. In the initial sales period, you will get a lot of objections and refusals. Welcome rejections and try being creative. It's the process of elimination of ways which don't work, that will guide you to your glory path.

Once you have found what works for you, you still won't be successful all the time, and that's where the significant learning comes – keep sharpening your axe. Be more aware of the change in customer psychology, about markets, about your approach, and learn from the top in your domain.

Sales experts are constant learners. They know the benefits of the products they sell and the services they offer. They are aware that their products enhance lives, and it is this very conviction that translates to enthusiasm when they share it with their customers. These emotions are infectious and generate momentum in the selling process. They never stop learning and improvising. Why is it you may wonder that these experts want to continue learning? You may think that they are at their peak with nothing more to achieve. But experts have reached their position because they comprehend that Sales is similar to the most intriguing game called Chess. It is one of the oldest board games with black and white squares with only 64 spaces and 16 pieces for each player.

There are 400 different positions after each player makes one move apiece. There are 72,084 positions after two moves by each player and 9+ million positions after three moves by each player. There are 288+ billion different possible positions after four moves apiece. There are more 40-move games on Level-1 than the number of electrons in our universe. There are more game-trees of Chess than the number of galaxies (100+ billion), and more openings, defenses, and gambits than the number of quarks in our universe! Chess is infinite. It does not depend just upon your game; there are many factors involved in it. The major factor is the other player. You have no clue as to what the other person is thinking, what moves the other person will make that can result in innumerable permutations, combinations, and strategies. That's what makes the game so similar to Sales. Right from the beginning of customer interaction, the permutations and combinations are infinite. Every word, every single aspect of body language, every choice has the power to change the outcome.

Imagine someone who wants to be a driver/chauffeur for passenger vehicles. This individual has read the instruction manual and has seen how people drive a car. He scores the highest in the written test. Now, I have a question for you. Would you entrust your life to him? The answer is a resounding No. WHY? You will tell me that he has no practical experience, and you have the right to be careful as you are going to entrust your life in his hands when you are a passenger in his vehicle.

Hence the driving test contains both a theoretical and practical element. The theory put into practice produces experience, which can make a good driver. Driving a car or any other vehicle is not an easy task as it requires focus, observation, thinking, and finally, the ability to coordinate all the actions to have a smooth and safe drive. While learning to drive, you may have found it an impossible undertaking. But as you practiced driving every day, you realized that you made each move without thinking over every step. When you finally became a certified driver, you were entirely on autopilot. Your actions had become an extension of your daily habit. You were a competent and careful driver, and this is why you refused to travel with the chauffeur who had only cleared the written test. You knew, too well, the importance of experience.

Experience makes all the difference between knowing something and having the skill to do it. Repetition is the password to mastering a skill, and there are no ways around it. Action is the only way to optimize your learning. It is not enough to dream as the dream has to turn into an action plan with goals in place. Taking care of the smallest details helps put the final picture into perspective. Repetition of skills creates an imprint in mind – our actions then become as involuntary as breathing. It becomes natural and not the result of a long contemplated response. If we adopt the same technique with sales and put those principles into practice, we develop our sales muscles. Remember, this is not a one-time activity as it requires you to change your former way of life and thinking. It is a self-exploratory process that necessitates an unsettling of conscious, unconscious, and conditioned beliefs that may be limiting your way of life and work. It has to be your decision to never settle for less, your choice to have the winner's title. This way of life, for continued success, depends upon a lot of commitment, dedication, and hard work. When these factors come together, they create the desired outcome.

Don't stop doing when you get it right. Keep honing your skills as the world evolves, and keep doing it till you can't get it wrong. Focus. Ask yourself why you do what you do? Why do you want to do something that you have never done? Your goal has to be precise. As the saying goes – If you want to achieve something you never had, you need to do something you have never done.

Get Out Of Your Comfort Zone.

As human beings, we are creatures of habit. We like to be in places of warmth and comfort, amongst family and friends. We have an inherent fear of moving out into the unknown as we live with negative 'What if' scenarios? We like to be with the familiar and avoid discomfort, and this state of mind breeds a complacent attitude. We need to step forward and choose to cross over to uncharted territory, realize and be aware that we need to continually expand our knowledge, increase our skillsets, and to gift ourselves a goldmine of possibilities.

The moment we get comfortable doing something, that is the moment when we need to rush out of our comfort zone and rise to the challenges posed by life, responding energetically and committing ourselves to a life of learning.

Great success stories have had humble beginnings and immense dedication.

Tinder & Alibaba physically traveled to their first users. Tinder went from 5,000 to 15,000 users by getting sorority girls to signup on the spot, while Alibaba 'brute-forced' its success by visiting factories one by one.

Quora & Reddit filled up their sites initially with their own content.

Dropbox & Threadless were the biggest believers in word-of-mouth marketing. While Dropbox launched shared folders and a massive referral campaign, Threadless let its community run their own initiatives.

OkCupid had legendary content on OKTrends and averaged 4,222 tweets per post. The content on OKTrends was so mindblowing that people despaired when it was discontinued.

Etsy harvested interest by reaching out to target communities on already established platforms.

Buffer got to 100k users primarily through frequent guest blogging.

Today they are huge names just because they moved out of their comfort zone and were committed to making their mark in the world.

So to be successful, begin with a positive mindset. Don't let your doubts tie you back. Your results will justify your courage and persistence. Stay on the course. Persevere.

To multiply your sales, an understanding of every single aspect of the sales process is necessary. Once we comprehend the various elements, we need to plan the implementation, then put the process in action, follow it with an evaluation and, tweak the approach to achieve maximum success. The right strategy, a critical mind, consistency, and confidence are crucial to take you to the next level. This book guides you on your path towards achieving extraordinary results. So let us embark on this exciting and happy journey to make the impossible, possible!

[TIME FOR ACTION]

Activity 1

1. Write down the names of effective salespeople that you know/have known
2. Write down what make/made them effective in sales
3. Get in touch with them and ask, "I want to be a successful sales professional like you, and need your assistance in understanding what makes you successful?"
4. Write down their responses and see if it matches with the answers you had written

Activity 2

Write down the answers to the questions (be as detailed as possible)

1. Why do you want to increase sales?
2. How will that impact your life next year?

3 How Is The World Of Sales Changing?

What can we do about it?

The Evolution Of Sales

To illustrate, let us imagine a scenario centuries ago. There were two people Ricka and Vega. Both were living their life with whatever items and resources they had and were able to procure. Ricka used to have surplus Rice, and Vega used to have surplus Vegetables. Eureka! They came up with the idea of exchanging the goods they had in excess (Barter System). Bartering refers to the trading of products and services.

"Be persistent. Go after what you want and enjoy doing it."

– Jill Konrath

Human wants and desires led to the creation of this excellent system, which was gratifying for some time. As the news spread, people started adopting this unique method of getting what they needed/wanted. While doing the barter, people discovered that some items (for example, cattle, grain, vegetables, sheep, fish, etc.) had more demand, and people started lining up for it (Supply and Demand).

Into this scenario, enters Fitch with an excess of fish and places Ricka in a dilemma. Should he barter his surplus rice for fish or vegetables? Vega and Fitch are also in competition as they need to reach a deal with Ricka and will try to sweeten the deal for getting rice. Ricka is at an advantage here as he has multiple products to choose from, and he is the only one with a product that others want. In essence, Buyer's Monopoly (Monopsony) suggests there is just a single buyer (who controls a large portion of the market) and multiple sellers.

Now let's change the dynamics in this market by introducing Rasmin, who has surplus rice and requires fish and vegetables. Now, the market has two suppliers of rice and market scenario changes. Ricka and Rasmin, both want to get their rice exchanged, and Vega and Fitch need the rice. In such a competitive market, apart from quality and price, trust and other unique, unseen parameters come into play. Increased number of buyers and sellers in the market make the dynamics complex, which necessitates the entry of Marketing and Selling into the game.

As time progressed, bartering transactions started taking time as people had to find someone with whom they could get a fair trade, which involved going to multiple people in different places – carrying their surplus goods. And it may not always be the case that what someone would require, would be present at that given time. There was a need for a solution to speed up the process, and hence 'Marketplace' and 'Currency' (animal skins, salt, etc.) came in circulation. The 'need-based trade' thus originated.

What has changed from then to now? Centuries later, moving with the times, we graduated to coins, paper currency, and virtual currency. The fundamentals have remained the same; however, the market has evolved. From the number of competitors to the number of products and services and, not to forget, the number of customers – everything has increased drastically. Businesses try to make profits and establish their presence in the market by offering something unique or selling uniquely, and enjoy the monopoly until a competitor appears.

These are the same principles and approach which we will build up in the coming chapters and make it more integrated with the sales approaches today. Growth of Small and Medium Enterprises (SMEs) has also affected the market dynamics. In the past, financing your own SME was very difficult if they did not have enough capital. In the absence of external funding for small and medium businesses, entrepreneurs had to take personal loans and invest it in their business, resulting in a very high cost of operations. As a consequence, business owners increased the price of their products to recover costs. If not, they had to bear the burden of substantial losses. In addition to these factors, these businesses had to hire exceptional salespeople at higher salaries to sell their products – which added to the OPEX (Operational Expenditure).

Furthermore, they were operating in a dynamic market in which there were similar products. Many businesses failed because they were unable to generate a steady, profitable sales funnel. As a result, banks were skeptical of providing loans to new ventures and made it even more difficult for SMEs to establish themselves. But things have changed now, and there is a tremendous opportunity for growth.

The following factors have been crucial in the astonishing growth of SMEs :

Credit From Financial Institutions

The easy availability of funding from banks and financial institutions has led to many people becoming entrepreneurs. With the availability of local and international investment as well as angel funding, SMEs have the best environment to flourish now.

Technology Has Helped To Reduce Capital And Operational Expenditure

Newer technologies enable enterprises to have faster seamless interactions with their customers and add value to the products they sell.

Government Initiatives To Offer A Subsidy For Enhancing The Economy And Increasing GDP

Today, many governments have modified their laws to encourage small businesses. The robust support of the government for this segment has seen it thrive beyond expectations. They have introduced bankruptcy laws that protect financial institutions from losses. Governments have also launched many initiatives to help small organizations cut down on taxes and operational costs. Due to government support, support from financial institutions, and angel investors, the market is flooded with SMEs today, leading to a tremendous increase in competition. With a finite income and a plethora of choices, marketing and brand building drives the 'supply and demand' market.

What role do the sales professionals play here? When the competition is absent, the salesperson's job is relatively easy. If the marketing is strong, customers will flock in, and the salesperson's job profile would be limited to answering questions and closing orders. It is when the competition surfaces, the role and scope of a salesperson change in extraordinary ways. Demanding customers have plenty of options to choose from, and hence the salespeople need to know and practice the science and art of professional selling. With the changing market scenarios, the roles of sales professionals have changed.

Let us look at two role-change barometers –

1) *Job Descriptions:* Many of you may have read through job descriptions of a salesperson in your career. A sneak-peek at some actual posts:

'We're looking for a results-driven sales representative to seek out and engage customer prospects actively. You will provide complete and appropriate solutions for every customer to boost top-line revenue growth, customer acquisition levels, and profitability.'

'Our company is looking for a Sales Representative to be responsible for generating leads and meeting sales goals. Duties will include sales presentations and product demonstrations, as well as negotiating contracts with potential clients. To be successful in this role, you will need to have a deep understanding of consumer behavior, human psychology, sales process and dynamics, and also superb interpersonal skills. Previous experience in a sales role is an advantage.'

This description followed by responsibilities and requirements. The job profile is not just about selling products; it is much more than that.

2) *Business Cards:* Some decades ago, sales professionals used to have designations like Sales Executive, Sales Manager, Sales Director, and the like. Today, sales professionals flaunt designations such as Client Servicing Executive, Key Account Manager, Senior Relationship Manager, Director Priority Banking, and so on. These designation changes have evolved in the last couple of decades. Have you ever wondered why these revisions? It is because of the word Sales.

Decades earlier, salespeople were considered extremely persuasive, talkative, scheming, and capable of pulling a fast one (stereotype). People believed that liars made better salespeople. Shocking, as it may sound, however, it is true. People have a propensity for judging individuals before meeting them – sometimes, solely in the light of what they do for a living. What's more unfortunate is that if you are a sales professional, people assume, more often than not, in the negative. Unless you can get past those biases, it will be harder than it should be for a salesperson. Therefore, we must create value for our customers, and if we don't, it is a misuse of the customer's time.

*Don't sell;
let people buy!*

[TIME FOR ACTION]

1) What is your job profile?

Write down what the organization expects from you. If you are an Entrepreneur, design your profile considering the Sales Part.

2) What else does your job profile include?

*This may be unstated in the job profile you have written down.

Why Did People Typecast Sales Professionals?

Think about the time when the first-ever mobile phones came into the market. Looking at the handset as a commodity with immense benefits and also as a status symbol, there was a tremendous desire to own the gadget, in addition to the excitement to see it, touch it, own it, and flaunt it. In that phase, the salespeople would have had a great time selling the product. There would have been an immense feeling of pride in doing so, as they were in constant demand. The handset company must have reaped in profits. History has proven that any success story is keenly followed, monitored, and scrutinized for replication – if they can do it, we can do it too. And as the competitors enter the market, the customers start getting diverted towards the new product. This situation creates a tough time for the salesperson as if customers don't come to buy, then the sales go down, and he/she needs to be creative and approach the customer. To achieve the target when selling is difficult, the only way forward is to Sell for Survival. The easiest way which many followed in this situation was to promise them the world and to give them a customer service number for complaints. People used to trust the salesperson only to realize later that they had lied to complete targets. There are many ways to falsify a sale. Though this brings immediate returns to the salesperson and organization, in the long run, the business loses a customer for life. Many people have experienced this several times in their life, and hence salespeople have been typecasted as liars.

Today if the business card carries the word Sales in the designation, the subconscious mind automatically suggests that this person is going to be talkative and will persuade me with false charm to buy something that I don't need. He will burn a hole in my pocket. This feeling is not a conscious one, it lies somewhere deep in the recesses of our mind, and it gets triggered by the word Sales.

This human psychology was causing issues in the sales domain, and someone came up with an excellent idea of changing the designation on the business card. Though these changes were cosmetic at first, they recreated the job profiles of salespeople. Salespeople are torchbearers of business. So we ought to take a different approach and try to understand this situation from an organization's perspective. Organizations face challenging times due to increased competition, and continuously struggle to establish market dominance for generating profits and ensuring sustainability. It is a constant quest for them to stand out in the market and get chosen over competitors.

Between 2000-2010, in the Telecom sector, a similar situation happened in India. There were more than ten telecom operators in a city, and to get a bigger slice of the market, they resorted to lowering the call rates by shifting from per-minute billing to per-second billing (as a differentiator) which sparked off a price war. Though this was beneficial to the customers, rather than helping the industry, it hampered their progress. Reason? There was a limit to how far they could cut down the prices. When the tariffs are plummeting, the ARPU (Average Revenue Per Unit) falls, and with increasing costs, the profit declines.

With lower margins, organizations had to reduce costs to still be in business. For businesses who were enjoying high-profit margins, it was not a matter of making profits any more – it was a matter of survival. And so began the trend of cutting costs and maximizing from the minimum.

Desperate situations called for desperate measures. When the price war set in motion, organizations had only two options to keep their market share – either provide exceptional service/quality and a differentiator or scale down the quality and enter the price war. If they chose to improve service/quality, it would mean an increase in their operating costs (which would translate to lesser profits initially). A delay caused in improving service or research for creating a differentiator would result in some competitor gnawing away at their market share, which would threaten their very survival. Many telecom companies opted to use and offer a lower quality of the equipment/materials/accessories to reduce costs, as that was the quickest way of staying in the game.

Businesses decided to let experienced people go and began hiring people with less experience and low salaries, still expecting an optimal performance from them. Every step taken in business has consequences, whether favorable or unfavorable. The race for a price drop to keep the market share had its effects too. By 2019, all the telecom companies in the city struggled to keep their heads over water. Many of the smaller organizations decided to either shut down operations or chose to merge. The major ones are now still fighting for creating another differentiator.

Hence it is crucial to understand:

- Employability and growth depends on profitable sales

- The price reduction may not be a sustainable strategy. The competition in the fastest time can always replicate price differentiator. A differentiator should set the stage for a profitable business.

Differentiators

Imagine that you are on vacation in Africa with your family and friends. You decide to go on a safari. Everyone is excited as the jeep starts moving when suddenly, the children spot a giraffe. They are so delighted to see one in real life. As the tour continues, they keep seeing more giraffes, but all of them look the same, differing only in size. The excitement that everybody had at the start of the journey dwindles as the novelty has worn off. You see the same giraffes all along the road, and you continue the trip with no further expectations. Everybody is bored, and they wait for the end of the journey.

Then suddenly, you hear kids screaming and shouting with joy. What have the children seen to make them react in such a manner? You look around, and you become speechless as this now seems to be a trip of a lifetime! You have seen the rarest of rare sights – A Rainbow Colored Giraffe!

How Is The World Of Sales Changing?

You are so astonished and surprised that you compel the driver to stop the vehicle so that you can capture this moment, pose for selfies with the Rainbow Giraffe in the background. The others also get down, and soon everyone is admiring the beautiful creature.

Now, if this were seen by a local with an entrepreneurial mindset, his mind would be filled with ideas. Maybe he could:

- Start a Selfie Point, arrange for a photographer and charge fees for clicking pictures
- Sell milk of the Rainbow Giraffe at a premium price
- Sell chocolates made of milk from Rainbow Giraffe
- Start 'Feed The Giraffe' counter
- Sell the exclusive story to media houses
- Sell souvenirs
- Sell clothing items with the picture of Rainbow Giraffe
- Sell advertising space at the spot (since a lot of footfall)
- Start a small eatery
- Sell Rainbow Giraffe stuffed toys for kids
- Color other Giraffes in individual color

The possibilities are endless! And each one of them is a unique business idea.

And for all you know, there was a mischievous kid at the safari park who had a lot of free time at hand and saw some paints and brushes and decided to color the Giraffe for sheer fun. Something unique presents a definite business opportunity.

Now, think of the multiple colors of the Rainbow Giraffe. Each color is unique yet adds to the overall beauty of the Rainbow Giraffe. Similarly, visualize the endless possibilities that lie in every business. It is the small unique differentiators that contribute to the big picture. Identify attributes that are in demand and set you apart from your competitors. If you are the only organization with a unique product offering, you will be able to attract a lot of new customers. A product with one-of-a-kind features, benefits, and service parameters helps a business to gain a definite competitive edge. You can create Million-dollar businesses if you can create a differentiator!

Customer Experience Cycle

Let's take the scenario of a company offering 'Car with Driver' service, and design a customer experience cycle for them.

The following are the stages:
- Customer Searching For Service
- Website Visit
- Booking
- Arrival On The Scheduled Date and Time
- Journey Experience
- Journey Completion

However, even when you look at each stage, there are 'Elements' in each stage.

Let's take an example of the 'Booking' stage. The elements would be:

- Ease of finding the booking link
- All booking related information present
- Simplicity of booking
- Different payment mechanisms
- Instant support incase any issues during booking
- Security of payment information
- Time taken for the booking
- Booking confirmation on the website
- Booking confirmation on Email/SMS

Similarly, for each Stage, there will be different Elements. Each Element can etch a WOW, Fair, or Ouch, in the subconscious mind and contribute to the overall experience. So if there are 7 Stages and an average of 10 Elements in each Stage, there are 70 opportunities to create an impression in the customer's mind. The more the WOWs, the more colorful the Giraffe, the better Brand Image, and Loyalty.

It becomes essential for any business to map the Customer Experience Cycle and craft a strategy for increasing the WOWs. From a sales perspective, it is vital to understand the Sales Experience Cycle and infuse opportunities to create a positive impression.

The Sales Experience Cycle begins with the initial contact, and ideally does not end unless the potential client does not have the possibility of being your customer. This cycle is essential for building a sales pipeline. Grow the list, engage with the list, and create WOWs.

Edward H. Chamberlin, in his book Theory of Monopolistic Competition, introduced the concept of product differentiation. A key sets you apart from your competitors in the market. Businesses that lack a product differentiator realize that it is close to impossible to survive in a competitive market.

Apple believed in Innovation as a differentiator. Disneyland believes in creating the most memorable experiences for visitors. Brands like Virgin, Montblanc, Google, Emirates Airlines, Starbucks, and many others believe in offering high standards of service to customers. For any business to remain profitable, they require new customers and, most importantly, to retain existing customers.

The telecom companies in the previous scenario made Price as a differentiator and faced the consequences. They learned their lessons, and now operators are trying to recover by focussing on offering unique differentiators such as highest data speed or network coverage. They have decided not to be a party to the price war and concentrate on other differentiators. The challenge is, will they be able to recover from losses?

[**TIME FOR ACTION**]

Benchmark against competition-

Write down key differentiators for:

    a) Your Product/Service

    b) Your Organization

    c) Your Customer Experience Cycle

    d) Your Personality and Inter-personal Skills

Customer Acquisition And Customer Retention

Customer Acquisition is the process of getting new customers for the business, and Customer Retention refers to the ability to keep customers and build their loyalty for sustained profits. Both are essential for business.

An existing customer is more valuable than a new one. The cost of acquiring a customer enables the business to determine the cost of the product/project. Customer Acquisition Cost (CAC) is the cost associated with convincing a consumer to buy your product or service, including research, product development, marketing, and advertising costs. CAC is an important business metric, and one should consider it along with Customer Lifetime Value (CLV). The calculation of customer valuation helps a company decide how much of its resources they can profitably spend on a particular customer.

What makes the CAC higher? The fact is that bringing in new customers is always difficult and expensive. Usually, people measure CAC based on the marketing expenditure versus customers acquired; however, that's inaccurate. To arrive at the exact cost of acquisition, we must also include other significant factors such as the Manpower Acquisition cost, CAPEX and OPEX, Lead Generation, Lead Nurturing, etc., to the marketing expenses. If the expense to acquire a new customer is high, the net profit decreases. A perfect balance is essential between CAC and Net Profits by keeping in mind the Vision and Mission of the organization. Customer acquisition is crucial, but we always need to keep the CAC, CLV, and Net profit in mind. Market research shows that it costs up to 5-7 times more to attract new customers than to keep an existing one. The longer the life cycle of an existing customer in business, the more profitable it becomes. So this becomes the priority for any organization to succeed. Considering a competitive market scenario, a mature organization should ideally have 65% of the revenue coming from existing customers and 35% from new customers. To get to this stage, the organization should do everything in its power for not losing its existing customers to competitors.

Taking customers for granted is the surest way of losing customers. Sometimes, satisfied customers do not return to do more business with the organization because they don't feel valued. In a world where technological advancement can bring competitive options closer, staying connected with the customer is crucial.

New organizations focus on getting new customers to increase their customer base, and the CAC can be extremely high if they expect faster growth. Getting customers is one thing; however, keeping them is another. If there is a lack of foundation to build sustainable relationships with customers, the CLV can decline drastically.

Whether it's a mature organization or a new organization, it becomes vital to build a stronger relationship with every customer. It is the key to survival, and hence traditional sales need to be replaced by consultative sales, which requires knowledge, experience, and expertise. Today's sales professionals need to break free from the conventional approach of Sales and look at it from a different angle, learn

How Is The World Of Sales Changing?

to build rapport with customers by sharing benefits and the value they will receive, and never push them to purchase the product or service. The salesperson needs to an expert regarding the product, competition information, the market situation as well as relationship-building techniques. A consultative salesperson never assumes, and would always ask excellent questions which help to get to the root of the problem, thereby making it easier to diagnose and provide a solution.

The consultative seller understands that questions can create a desire to seek solutions and is willing to risk asking 'seemingly uncomfortable' questions as that will lead to useful advice on resolving the issue. The professional salesperson looks not only at organizational expectations and profits for initial sales but also at building customer trust and rapport for repeat sales.

Sales Targets	Consultant
Marketing Products	Trusted Resource
Profitable Negotiations	Great Communicator
Representing Brand	Effective Planner
Customized Sales Strategy	Business Supporter
Time management	Industry Expert
Customer Feedback	Product Expert
Market Feedback	Innovator

MAJOR EXPECTATIONS FROM A SALES PROFESSIONAL

There is a tightrope that a professional salesperson needs to walk on to balance the organizational expectations and customer expectations.

To be able to manage both, the salesperson should create and maintain a lasting relationship with a customer, thus ensuring repeat profitable business in a competitive environment.

> *The success mantra for experienced sales professionals is – Learn to unlearn and re-learn! That is the only way to be successful. Price is usually an issue in the absence of value*

This process requires time, efforts, and commitment to building on the existing knowledge and establishing oneself as a sales professional.

If not, there will be a competitive threat from your peers and other sales professionals from your competitor organizations. Today, the fresh flow of talent pouring into organizations, are adaptable, having access to updated knowledge as well as learnings from global case studies.

Learning is easy for new salespeople because they start with a tabula rasa – a blank slate.

[TIME FOR ACTION]

Let's do some number crunching. Input the numbers next to each field.

Parameters	Figures
Annual Turnover Of Organization (A)	
Number Of Customers (B)	
Average Revenue Per Customer (B/A)	
Number Of Customers Gained In Last Year (N)	
Average Revenue From New Customers (RA)	
Number Of Existing Customers (E = B-N)	
Average Revenue From Existing Customers (RE)	
Percentage Of New Customers (N/B) %	
Percentage Of Business From New Customers (RA/A) %	
Percentage Of Existing Customer (E/B) %	
Percentage Of Business From Existing Customers (RE/A) %	
From The Existing Customers, How Many Did You Lose In The Last Year?	
What Was The Approximate Revenue Loss Because Of Customers Leaving?	

Try to get accurate details. It might require investing time and efforts, however it will yield interesting insights.

You can do this for yourself/your team as well and start benchmarking performance.

For more insights, track this for:

    a. Product Segment

    b. Region

    c. Country

Based on the answers, you may want to examine the following questions:

- Who is bringing you more revenue, New or Existing customers?
- What are the ways by which you can increase the revenue for new customers?
- What are the ways you can increase the revenue from existing customers?
- What measures can you take to stop customers from leaving?

Customer Segmentation And Category Sales Approach

If the organization has a one size fits all approach for the existing customers, then not all customers are going to be happy. Some of them may be heavy spenders, some may be regular buyers, and that approach can cause bigger damage. Hence the sales professionals need to design their approach and strategy based on customer segmentation.

Similar to the BCG Growth matrix, which is for products, a 'Segmentation Strategy Matrix' needs to be made for existing customers.

For this you need :

- List of customers you are accountable for
- Per year billing (taken as an average)
- No. of transactions per year (taken as an average)

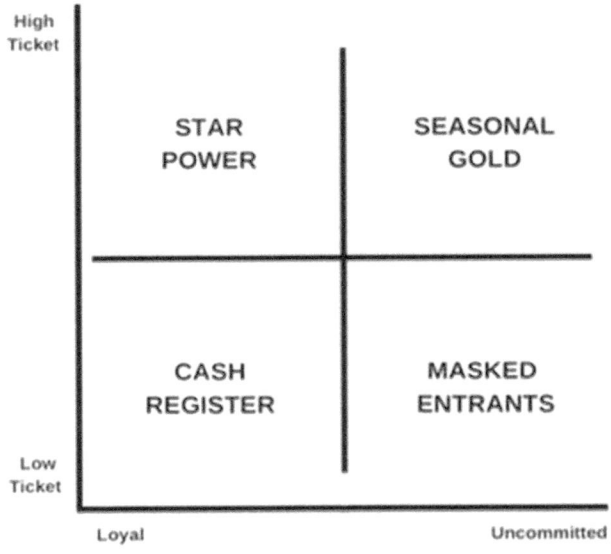

Based on this, categorize them as in the below matrix.

Let us look at each category and design a strategy for them.

Star Power – High Ticket Sales And Loyal (Repeat Buyers)

Who Are They?

Depending on the nature of the business, Around 50% of the billing is done by them. They are your Key Accounts, and you would always want them to be with you. They have the Star Power to make your organization grow. Since they have the Star Power, your competitors are eyeing them too, and they will put in relentless efforts to put the foot in the door first and try and snatch business. For you, a loss of even one such client can drastically hamper your target achievement.

Your Strategy:

During my masterclass, most people said giving discounts, and unbeatable prices would deter Star Powers from moving. However, John Gattorna conducted a now-famous study while he was a visiting professor at Macquarie Graduate School of Management in 2008 and found the following distribution for why businesses lose customers:

4% Natural attrition (e.g. moved away, passed on, etc)

5% Referred to a competitor by their friend or relatives

9% Competitive reasons – mostly price

14% Product/service dissatisfaction (quality)

68% Perceived indifference or rude behavior

So the objective should not be luring them with reduced prices. They like your products/services, and they see the value; hence they are paying for it. Price is not the challenge here.

There will be times when the competition will offer them a lower price, and they will tell you about it. It's during these times that you need leverage. Your objective is to make profitable sales – always remember that discounting is not the option.

If ABC, your competitor, had approached your Star power, their objective would be to steal a deal under your nose, and they would be willing to provide your client more than what you are offering. So they would give reduced pricing, and if you match it, ABC will still reduce the pricing. If you give extra considerations, ABC can deliver that as well. The battle can continue, and you will get in the survival mode, while ABC will have nothing to lose.

So the strategy is to build walls around Star Powers, which are impenetrable by competition.

Think of all the things that you could do to strengthen the bond. The stronger the relationship, the more difficult it is for them to move away. Always show the value that you would bring to them.

One of the participants in my session used this learning for fantastic leverage. He is a Key Account Manager for a reputed Hotel, and his Star Power client is from the IT domain. He uses 'Google Alert' service to know about the advancements in the IT domain, and shares the relevant information with the key people in the Star Power company, thus adding value. Also, he has set alerts for the company and leadership team of the company. Whenever the company or its products get mentioned in the digital world, he receives an alert to act on. If they announce a new product, he checks for the support they would require from his side. If they win an award or a contract, he sends them a card or a bouquet to congratulate them. It helps him to be a part of their professional family.

One organization arranges a Networking party for their Star Powers to facilitate inter-business within them; if their business grows, yours does too!

One organization has reserved parking for Star Power Customers, which is covered and next to the CEO's parking spot.

One Key Account Manager keeps track of birthdate, anniversary date, children's birthdates, their exam and results dates, and important cultural dates of all the key people from the Star Powers.

Seasonal Gold – High Ticket Sales And Occasional Buyers

Who Are They?

Depending on the business, they usually contribute to 20% to the turnover. It's interesting to find out that despite having funds, why are they buying occasionally?

The most probable answers are:

1. They are someone else Star Powers, and when their requirements are not met, they turn to you. So you are their Plan B
2. They genuinely don't have a regular need, and when they do, they approach you

Your Strategy:

So the first step would be to find out what the scenario is with them and plan the way forward. If it's the first reason, then understand what makes them go to your competition. Is it because they experienced poor service or rude behavior from your employees (68%), or they are dissatisfied with the quality (14%), or they have a long-standing relationship with the competition and are reluctant to change (5%)?

If it's because of poor service, then you need to try and make up for it, go beyond your normal service levels, and make them feel special. Building confidence and trust are essential. Get them used to you and keep them hooked by adding value.

Imagine a Seasonal Gold turning into Star Power. Think of the revenue they will be bringing in per year. How would that affect your targets and incentives?

If it's the second reason,

Then you may want to have a look at their growth plan, see if there is anything that you can do to aid their growth. Remember, if you are adding value to them, they will stick with you.

Remember – If their business grows, so does yours!

Turn the Seasonal Gold into Gold Mines.

Cash Registers – Low Ticket Sales And Loyal

Who Are They?

Cash registers keep the cash flow going for business. They purchase frequently from you. They don't have high requirements, hence the low ticket sales. They are very loyal and will rarely shift to competition, and usually contribute to 20-25% of the revenue. Since they generate regular cash flow, which can take care of Operational Expenses, they are considered important.

Your Strategy:

The strategy is to keep growing the customer base. Keep track of churn (number of customers leaving you) and new additions (number of customers joining you). Calculate the percentage of Cash Registers in your business and the Average Revenue they are generating. Keep the proportion in mind when you are looking at yearly targets, as they will play a significant role in sales forecasting. Invest in growing the base through sustained marketing efforts. Use SMS, Emails and Social Media for increasing engagement. Don't spend lot of time and lot of money. Work smart to tap into newer markets and keep growing this base. Be mindful of the Customer Acqusition Costs for Cash Registers and plan your Marketing Budget accordingly. Develop products which appeal to them. Since they generate regular cash flow, you need to keep an eye on their behavior and trends.

Masked Entrants – Low Ticket Sales And Occasional Buyers

Who Are They?

Masked entrants fall into two categories:

1. Those whom you are pursuing (who have never purchased from you)
2. Those who are trying out your product or service

Your Strategy:

Masked entrants are critical in your business. Even for a healthy net profit organization, it is essential to pursue them and focus on bringing the fresh blood in your system. With the increasing competition, there will always be some of your existing customers who would decide to move out, which can result in lower turnover and profits. They usually contribute to 5%-10% of the revenue; however, the time dedication for such customers should be more. An experienced Sales professional should always aim to get 20% new customers on board.

Most sales professionals focus on overall sales and pay little attention to the Category Sales Approach. Initially, time and effort are required to pull out the data and categorize; however, it is immensely beneficial for exceeding sales targets.

[TIME FOR ACTION]

- Get a list of your customers, get the data of the number of purchases made, the first purchase date, last purchase date, Revenue per purchase, and highest order placed
- Use the data to classify customers into four categories
- Decide a target and strategy for each category
- Make a list of action items for each category
- Plan a monthly calendar
- Identify the resources required for the activities
- Plan the work, and work the plan

4 What Are The Buying Motivators?

How to boost your sales?

Dangers And Danglers

"Why people buy?' is an intriguing question, the reasons manifold. What are the reasons people and organizations buy specific products and services? What makes them exchange their hard-earned money for what you are offering? What drives them to see your products and services as something of value? What benefits appeal to them? Let us start with you. Think about your last purchase, what did you purchase and why? Now think about something that you bought for yourself, and it was an absolute necessity. Do you sometimes buy luxury items that you can live without? Are you

> *"Enchantment is the purest form of sales."*
>
> – Guy Kawasaki

fulfilling your need or a want? Where would you draw the line between a need and a desire?

People buy for different reasons, called 'buying motivators' – anything that persuades you to buy is a buying motivator. Why do you buy a new phone? Let us take a walk down memory lane. Which mobile/cell phone do you have now and what made you buy it.

The answers could be:

- New technology/version upgrade
- Attractive looks
- Multiple features
- Best and most sought after brand
- My favorite brand
- Economical – fits my budget
- The present phone has technical issues (phone freezes, hangs)
- At a discounted rate making it a sensible purchase
- A friend has it/peer pressure
- Sense of achievement
- The salesperson convinced me
- The phone fits in my hand
- Retail therapy
- My family member wanted it
- It was necessary (need)

- It saves me time (time saver)
- It is a status symbol
- ....

During one of my brainstorming sessions with a group, they came up with 103 different reasons for purchasing a product! We decided to categorize them.

1. More: Saving or Acquiring money, Durability, etc.
2. Comfort/Pleasure: Beauty Enhancement, Good Health, Enjoyment, Recreation, Beauty Enhancement, etc.
3. Love And Affection: Admiration, Security, Social Approval, etc.
4. Fear Of Loss: Prevent Loss, Safety, No Blame, Loss of Time, etc.
5. Avoidance Of Issue: Relief from Pain, Less Work, No Worry, Avoiding Quarrels
6. Pride & Prestige: Status Symbol, Style, Recognition, Imitation etc.

But if you take a closer look at the six groups, you will notice that they primarily come down to just two fundamental categories.

Category 1: Dangers

This category includes all the reasons to avoid any danger or pain. If someone's phone has constant technical issues, then that's a pain area. If the phone does not fit in hand, that's discomfort. If it does not support specific technology that is necessary for everyday life, then that is an issue. So any motivator which can reduce discomfort falls in this category.

Category 2: Danglers

This category includes all the reasons that give us pleasure. Reasons which gratify our aspirations – for example, a phone becomes a status symbol if it is an elite brand. If the phone has advanced features and applications, then it enriches the quality of life.

So why do people buy? People buy for only two reasons – to eliminate the current or future danger or to enrich the quality of life. Having this knowledge alone is not helpful; one needs to use that knowledge and increase sales. It is essential to understand the 3 step ISP process –

1. Identify the buying reason
2. Set the stage
3. Position the product

How vital is each step?

Stage 1 – Identify (Importance Level: 50%)

The reasons people buy things are manifold, and this can be mindboggling for a salesperson. The motives can be internal or external. Determining why people purchase any product or service is the first step in increasing your sales. The salesperson must be able to recognize buying habits and the various factors that contribute to it. If you are unable to identify the buying reason, then the sale process has very little chance of success.

There are three types of prospects/customers:

1. One who is aware of his/her problem and is actively seeking to resolve it
2. The second has some idea that he/she has an issue but is unsure of what to do about it. The consequences, in the absence of a solution, does not hold much importance. The 'problem' is not on their priority list
3. And, finally, the customer who is not conscious of the issue at hand, or does not realize that there is a solution to better their situation Appropriate probing questions will help you identify the type, and then the process of matchmaking begins. Depending on the type, the time taken for the sale may vary. For someone who is actively looking for the solution, the sale time can be lesser as compared to someone who does not know the potential danger or dangler.

Stage 2 – Set Stage (Importance Level: 30%)

People do not like being sold to; they do like to buy. In this stage, don't talk about the product, talk about the potential loss if the product is not purchased. You will make them realize what their 'Danger' will be if they don't buy. In case their buying motivator is 'Pleasure,' then talk about how they would benefit by choosing the product.

One of the organization DOKA, for whose salespeople had attended my session, grabbed a major contract by implementing this. DOKA, a world leader in formworks, had a potential client, an organization that was handling a massive construction project and needed formwork. The client was keener on price than quality. DOKA couldn't match the price as their product quality was the best in the region, and it seemed that they would lose the contract. Since the deal was worth millions of dollars, the Key Account Manager handling the account still pursued the discussions and got to know that the construction will happen in the night time, and they would require the delivery of materials during night time only. The competitor offering the low price was unable to do that, and that became the selling point. The Key Account Manager was able to get the multi-million dollar contract at a profitable price point.

The key to success is to differentiate the product or associated service from the multitudes available in the market. Questioning for identifying the Danger and Dangler needs to happen on the lines of efficiency, and not on the product in general. In a B2B model, 'Credit Period' or 'After Sales Service' or any other factor can be a key area for setting the stage.

Stage 3 – Position Product (Importance Level: 20%)

In this stage, you will introduce the product or service as a solution. You must resist the impulse of giving your customers something to oppose. Take their side by empathizing with them and let them know that you understand their position.

When you do this, the customer has nothing to oppose or reject. They start listening to you with a keen ear as opposed to just hearing you. The customer agrees with you and feels that both of you share the same thought process. They don't think that someone is selling them something.

It is essential to share the benefits of the product and how the benefits will help to overcome challenges or obstacles faced by the customer. This end game relies on one of the fundamental pillars of Sales – F. A. B.

F – Features

A – Advantages

B – Benefits

Understanding Of Fab

What Is A Feature?

Let's take the example of a Mobile Handset and identify features.

- The size of the mobile is 7 inches
- The mobile hast two cameras
- The handset has a touch screen
- The handset is gold in color
- The handset is dual SIM

A feature is something that the product has, or product is and is non-debatable. These are facts, and no one can dispute that. Similar to the mobile, your product or service will also have many features. It is essential to list down all the features of your product or service.

Impossible Sales

What Is An Advantage?

Anything which a Feature is capable of doing is an Advantage.

Let's look at the features above and position them as an advantage.

1. The size of the mobile is 7 inches
   - The mobile could easily fit into your pocket or handbag.
   - The screen size makes the viewing easy

2. The mobile has 2 cameras
   - You can take selfies with ease

3. The handset is a touch screen
   - Looks elegant
   - Easy to use
   - You get a bigger screen as the keypad reduces the screen size

4. It's a Gold color handset
   - Handset looks royal
   - Can go with any outfit or accessory

5. The handset is dual SIM

    - You can have a business number and a personal number simultaneously
    - Saves money

These advantages are the *potential benefits* for a customer

What Is A Benefit Then?

A Benefit is an advantage that is useful for a customer. Make these benefits easy to spot and convert the product's features into indispensable (problem-solving) assets. Match desires and features. Translate a luxury into a necessity, something that the customer must have.

If you know that a customer is an international traveler, then you could look at these points:

1. Golden Color
2. Dual SIM
3. 2 Cameras

These are anticipated *Lines Of Approach* as they may appeal to the customer. Anticipate motivations and target needs/aspirations.

For example:

The golden color of the mobile could have different connotations for the customer. It could make them feel like royalty, act as a status symbol, and simultaneously look good with any attire.

A dual SIM feature would help the customer to have a local number as well as an international number activated on the same phone in place of carrying two phones. It would also help avoid loss of opportunities and other advantages due to missed calls on a single SIM phone.

Two cameras on a mobile phone would eliminate the need to carry a separate camera for taking selfies or taking photographs while sight-seeing.

However, these are still Lines of Approach. Until you understand what appeals to the customer, or what the customer prefers, it is still not a benefit statement.

One needs to be sure about customer preferences (identify stage) before jumping in to share the benefits. Since buying is logical as well as an emotional decision, one needs to connect with the customer by understanding their needs/wants.

Now let's analyse a sample conversation between Dana (Customer) and Mark (Sales Professional):

Dana: *"I am looking for a handset."*

Mark: *"Great, you have come to the right place. We have a wide range of handsets, and I am sure we can find one that's best suited for your requirements. May I ask what the prime reason/purpose is?"*

Dana: *"Well, I am fed up with my handset. It hangs most of the time and has some scratches on it."*

Mark: *"Many customers have voiced similar issues. Do you think it is because of using multiple applications or storage issues?"*

Dana: *"I don't know. I do use a lot of applications simultaneously."*

Mark: *"May I see the handset? (After Examination) This model has a 1 GB processor, and that's why when you use multiple applications, it tends to be very slow. The scratches dull the attractiveness of the handset. How did these scratches come about?"*

Dana: *"Well, that happens when you have dogs at home."*

Let's analyze the conversation – so far, no product is pitched. The price has not come into the picture. In an amicable, conversational manner, Mark has asked questions that have identified two Dangers. There could be more too. Uncovering Dangers and Danglers is an art. Is it easy? No, it is not. It takes a fair amount of practice to get the questioning techniques right. One of the books which elaborate on this approach is SPIN Selling. It's a Pull based approach instead of a Push Approach.

If Mark has a thorough knowledge of the product's features, then it is easier for him to identify a handset that matches the requirements of the customer – in short, a handset which has larger processing power, and a scratch-resistant screen. But before that, he needs to be sure about the line of approach and create value for the need.

The conversation could go like this –

Mark: *"In a world where new apps get launched every day, it is of utmost importance that the handset supports their effective use. Don't you think so? Apart from the optimum performance of the phone and being scratch-resistant, would you like to go with the same color, or do you want to try something different?"*

Dana: *"I wouldn't mind a different color."*

Mark: *"Great! Let's have a look at some of the options."*

One needs to understand that your product or brand needs to be picked from the many options which are screaming *"Pick Me, Pick Me!"* Creating a product worth buying is one aspect, but creating a marketable product is the priority. When you sell or market your product, identify what Dangers could it solve and what Danglers could it target. Build a marketing campaign that addresses the audience profile. As Mark shows us, the strategy should be based on the benefits and the impact you plan to have on your potential customers. That should be the sales professional's purpose.

Tele-brands or similar channels use one of the classic examples of this strategy. You may have seen the advertisement featuring a weight loss product or formulas that increase your height or make your skin fairer or a kitchen device that can help you cut vegetables faster or the likes of it.

Well, let us take a cursory look at a weight loss advertisement. What is the first thing you see? Is it the product and the services it offers? Is it the cost of the product? No, none of that.

You see a person saying something similar to this:

"I was fat. People used to make fun of me all the time. They called me fatso. I had no social life. Girls would not talk to me. I could not fit in my clothes. Travelling was a pain. I had developed some health problems because of my excess weight. I was depressed all the time. I had no life! I was ready to give up on everything that mattered to me. Then I heard the words 'Super Fat Burner' on TV. In the beginning, I watched the presentation with little interest. But as I continued listening, I was surprised to learn how it had changed people's lives; I decided to try it. Here I am now, and I want to share my success with you. This is THE product which changed my life – just two tablets a day, and I lost 50 lbs in only 2 months. My clothes started fitting me. My friends were surprised at the transformation. People were attracted to the new me. I began to socialize and soon was the center of attention in my friend circle."

The screen shows an image of an obese person and then a fit and slimmer version of the same person. Then there are testimonials from others who have tried the product and have benefitted from it. After three testimonials, the first person is back again and says, *"If you also want to change your life, and get rid of your health problems, get the 'Super Fat Burner' now."* On the screen appears an attractively packaged product with the figure $500. Then the price is crossed out, another price flashes $ 300 (which gets crossed out too), and a price of $150 comes up. It is followed by a

Buy 1 get 1 Free offer. So the valid price is 'just' $75 ONLY. It is followed by a call to action and the ringing of the phone – saying this is a limited time offer, and the phone lines are open. If you order at that instant, you can get the product delivered to your doorstep in the next 48 hours.

Have you ever seen or purchased a product like this? If so, what did you feel, and why did you buy it? Let us have a look at the presentation of this product.

Did you notice the time is this advertisement generally telecasted? Have you paid attention? Usually, after lunch or dinner time. What do you think could be the reason for the timing? Any guesses? Well, it is quite simple. The advertisement targets people with weight issues, and people who have a heavy lunch or dinner are already in the mindset that they have eaten a lot. And it is easier to target them at their weakest moment when they feel guilty of having eaten/consumed a lot. Another reason for the timing is that after lunch or dinner, the blood flow in the body is diverted to the stomach to aid in the digestion of food, making the person less capable of making rational decisions. So that's how timing works in sales and marketing!

Let's analyze the format for the sales pitch, which is an exceptionally well crafted One-Way Sales Pitch.

Step 1 – Connection – Past And Present

The start of the advertisement is a 'Connect' – by identifying a situation that the target audience may have faced. Have you heard of the saying – 'Birds of a feather flock together'?

Well, if I am a fat person, and I see a person on TV saying that he was obese, it automatically translates to the fact that he WAS overweight (in the past), and now he is NOT. That's a trigger to the subconscious indicating how the product has transformed a dull past into a bright present, moving towards a sparkling future. This is something that the viewer must have thought of a million times every day.

Now, this is the 'Connect' in the advertisement.

Step 2 – Issues Awareness

Different 'Dangers' are used here.

- Humiliation – People used to make fun of me all the time
- Love and Belongingness – Girls wouldn't talk to me
- Money and Time – Buying new clothes because clothes wouldn't fit
- Sustainability – Health conditions

Step 3 – Magic Offering

Different 'Danglers' are used here.

A product was introduced to the customer and the many ways in which it has benefited the person. Some of the crucial points to note –

- Ease – Only two tablets per day
- No Effort – Not going to the gym, thus saving time and energy

- Cost-Effective – price reduced three times and an attractive offer if you order now

Step 4 – Trust Through Testimonials

Testimonials are used to gain Trust. The effect is psychological. It is the Mass Effect – that moment when you hear many people endorsing a product because it has worked for them, and you tend to see how you, too, can gain from the positive outcome it offers. There is a call to action – Call Now.

Step 5 – Action Required

The words – 'Phone lines' signify to the subconscious mind that it's not just one person attending the call; there are many people present to take the calls and take orders. This indicates that many callers are convinced of the effectiveness of the product and its solution. So the subconscious mind registers that this product is in high demand. Sometimes the offer is only for a limited time, which instills a fear of loss – if the product is not bought within the time limit.

So the model used is:

- C – Connect: Past and Present
- I – Issue Awareness
- M – Magic Offering
- T – Trust Through Testimonials
- A – Action Required

The CIMTA model is great for a One-way Sales Pitch, and the success of this sales model can be measured by the number of channels in different countries, advertising numerous products. In some countries, there are dedicated channels that broadcast only these advertisements 24/7. Imagine the amount of revenue generated!

This model works on the anticipation of problems faced and the possible desire for solutions. It is a very insightful model that targets the Dangers and the Danglers in Sales. Organizations who are yet to create their brand as a buying motivator, generally thrive on this model. Whether the products or the approach is good or bad is subjective and is a matter of perception; however, the model is result-oriented.

The psychology of buying and the psychology of selling are deciding factors in any business. Let us review what we have discussed.

- People buy for different reasons, and hence it is imperative to look at a sale from the buyer's point of view. It is essential, as salespeople, to understand the buyer's perspective and comprehend that people make these decisions based on both emotional impulses as well as logical facts.

- While making buying decisions for themselves, consumers will typically think about how they can benefit by purchasing a particular product. It is crucial to answering the consumer's WIIFM – 'What's in it for me?', from their perspective.

- The underlying element in a successful sale is the establishment of a credible and trustworthy relationship. When people like you, they will listen to you; they will buy when they trust you. Consumers need to see the salesperson as someone who has their best intention at heart.

- People buy because they anticipate happiness or relief. And they are ready to give away something for another that is of more value to them now. Value is relative. It is contingent on what the buyer will benefit from and how much cost is he/she willing to bear. Hence the salesperson needs to uncover the tangible and intangible benefits which contribute to the value.

- Buyers usually need an assurance of products and services, especially in a B2B scenario, since the price point is upwards. You must be able to demonstrate how a particular product has helped people or organizations.

[TIME FOR ACTION]

For any one of your product/service, write down at least 5 Features:

1) _____

2) _____

3) _____

4) _____

5) _____

Now take any 3 Features, and for each Feature identify the possible Advantages.

Some Features can have just one Advantage, and some may have multiple Advantages.

*Some Features can have more than 3 Advantages.

Feature 1:

Advantage a:

Advantage b:

Advantage c:

Feature 2:

Advantage a:

Advantage b:

Advantage c:

Feature 3:

Advantage a:

Advantage b:

Advantage c:

Now mark the Advantages which you think can be used to solve the most difficult or common problems (Dangers) for potential customers. If you find it challenging to identify the Dangers, then look for the Danglers. There will always be some buying motivators. If you can't find, put on your 'creative hat' and re-look, or ask for ideas from people in the same domain.

When you are interacting with the client, these are the 'lines of questioning approach' you should be following.

For each product or service, this one time activity which will bring you a lot closer to your seemingly impossible targets.

Up-Selling & Cross-Selling

Too many opportunities are lost for fear of rejection. Over the years, our minds have been primed by the line A bird in the hand is worth two in the bush, hence salespeople feel that if they decide to up-sell or cross-sell, they might lose the current sale. If the selling processes involves identifying the Danger or Dangler, then the customer is going to be all ears to your next value proposition.

Up-Selling is when you offer a:

- Premium product instead of the standard
- More quantity of same product
- Bigger size

Cross-Selling is when you offer:

- A related product to work in collaboration with existing product
- A different product or service

The most common example of Up-selling and Cross-selling is experienced at McDonalds when they ask:

Would that be Medium or Large? (Upselling)

Would you like fries/Coke with that? (Cross-Selling)

Effective Up-Selling and Cross-Selling requires careful timing, listening skills, and practicing restraint.

Some tips:

- Up-sell or Cross-sell only when the customer has decided to purchase. If done before 'selling' the main product, it will scare or confuse the customer.

- Be reasonable and consider the customer's budget. Don't let the additional purchase look like a major purchase.

- Make sure the Up-sell or Cross-sell is adding real value, and it's not just something that is increasing your profit or reducing your inventory.

5 Are You A Sales Hitter, Cultivator Or Trapper?

What is the best blend?

Hitters And Cultivators In Sales

Does this story resonate with the sales work profile today? I can see you nodding in agreement. There might be a few instances where the story diverges, but the plot remains the same. Let us define and discuss hitters and cultivators in the present-day sales scenario.

"The measure of intelligence is the ability to change."

– Albert Einstein

The Hitter:

A hitter usually stands out from the crowd, is more alert, and displays confidence to tackle any type of customer or situation. They have high energy and often inspire people around them. They constantly search, recognize, and capitalize on new opportunities. They would go after new prospects in the previously undefined territory. Hitting for new clients is routine, in the absence of which a business can fail. They approach prospective customers and convince them to partner and purchase the products they are selling. Even if most responses are negative, they still keep their chin up and go about fulfilling their responsibilities. When faced with seemingly mammoth tasks, the Hitters go out on the field, watch out for potential customers, engage with them, and strike at the opportunity. These people are friendly, outspoken, courageous, risk-takers, adventurous. Sometimes they win, and often they face nothing but rejection. But for them, the show goes on. Hitters focus only on the opportunities. Everything else is a distraction. They get new business, work in new sales territories, concentrate on turning prospects into customers, and don't mind pushing for a close when they recognize a window of opportunity.

The Cultivator:

The cultivator seemingly has it much more comfortable than the hitter. They nurture relationships and extract opportunities within the available customer base in the company. This role is indispensable. The cultivator faces less rejection when his clients are aware of his honesty and his track record, and best interests at heart. The cultivator comprehends human psychology, has learned about the customer's choices, before positioning the products based on his knowledge of preferences.

Cultivators develop long-term customer relationships, nurture them, knowing that the result will come later. They focus on building connections and getting business out of the relationships built. Cultivators are adept at identifying, analyzing, and solving client issues and most often design custom solutions keeping the customer's needs at heart. They are excellent at sustaining customer loyalty because they pay enormous attention to detail. They accomplish their administrative duties conscientiously. Word of mouth publicity works for them.

The Trapper:

In the jungle, a Trapper attracts the prey by placing bait in the trap i.e., cheese to catch the mice or honey for the bears, etc. Trappers never pursue; They attract! In a business organization, the Trapper is most likely associated with the marketing department. But he/she is also closely linked to the sales division. A Trapper does not chase for prospects as much as a Hunter. A Trapper enjoys determining the market, finding prospects, and crafts the right message to reel them in.

So, what is the approach that we must adopt? Sales departments and sales professionals always ask themselves this question. Should they base their choice on size and type of the company, or the number of years in the business, or type of product or service offered? Would the personality of the sales professionals determine the approach or that of the customers?

Let us have a look at various factors that can influence this decision.

1) Organizational Age And Strategy

If the organization is new with limited access to finances for sustainability, then the immediate requirement is to get customers who could propel the business forward. At this stage, a Trapper and Hunter role is essential.

2) Your Objective In The Organization

What is your role? Is it to bring new customers? Or to extract more business from existing customers? Are you required to create and build a brand image? What is the percentage of business expected from New versus Existing customers? The answers would help deter the approach.

3) Product Type – Ready To Sell Or Customized

If your product is Ready-To-Sell, then you could choose the Hitter approach. However, if it is tailor-made, you would require a Cultivator approach to gain trust and then develop a custom solution based on requirements.

4) Product Life Cycle – Time In Market

During the introduction stage, the sales depend on the 'uniqueness' of the product. Finding the right target audience generally happens through marketing – a Trapper approach. However, for the buy-in and closing the deal, one needs to adopt the Hunter approach.

During the Growth Stage, when organizations realize that the product is marketable, and more salespeople are needed to capitalize on the monopoly, Hitters are essential for maximizing the profits and increase the market share.

Maturity and Decline require a Cultivator approach dominantly as this is the gap through which competitors have gained access to the business and are dividing your market share. This time, the relationship-building approach works as it will not let the customers slip away.

In the Decline phase of the product lifecycle, organizations either need to upgrade their offering or create a new marketable product, and thus a new Product Life Cycle (PLC) starts! This is called an Extension Phase. One of the organizations which use PLC effectively is Apple. When the existing product has reached the maturity stage, Apple has been introducing new models.

Traditionally, a salesperson's profile would indicate the requirement of a Hitter or a Cultivator approach. However, in today's world, the lines are blurred. If a Hitter has Cultivator skills, it would be easy to get referrals from previous clients. Some sales professionals hold the responsibility of handling major client accounts, and they need to cultivate relationships well. However, if these professionals can't 'Hit' the right kind of influencers or decision-makers and close the requirement with them, then all the efforts put in for the cultivation are practically useless. So, ideally, a sales professional must adapt to being a Trapper, Hitter, as well as a Cultivator as the situation demands. Remember, businesses need profits to survive, and profits come from selling products or services.

[TIME FOR ACTION]

1. What is your preferred or natural sales personality – Trapper, Hitter, or Cultivator?

2. Considering your job profile, what percentage of personality mix is ideally required?

3. What knowledge or skills do you need to have to enhance your Trapper, Hitter, and Cultivator Personality?

4. What steps would you take to accomplish that?

6 How Does a Sales Cycle Help You?

How do you make one ?

Success Loves Preparation

Some years ago, during one of my business consulting assignments, I was talking to Simone, who is an entrepreneur in India. The objective was to find ways to increase business for her.

After the initial pleasantries were exchanged, we immediately got down to business. My objective was to gauge the current and expected level of growth.

"The difference between a successful person and others is not a lack of strength, not a lack of knowledge, but rather a lack of will."

– Vince Lombardi

How Does A Sales Cycle Help You?

The conversation went like this:

I: *"What's your target achievement for next year?"*

Simone: *"I want to achieve INR Ten Million."*

I: *"How much did you make in last year?"*

Simone: *"It was nearly INR 2 Million."*

That's a steep growth, and I wanted to know whether she had a plan in mind and followed up with a volley of questions:

- *What's the average earning per recruitment?*
- *How many recruitments have you done in the last year?*
- *How many repeat customers do you have?*
- *What's the average number of recruitments per NEW client?*
- *How much time does it take to gain the first business from a new client?*
- *How frequently does an existing client request for your services?*
- *How many major competitors do you have currently?*
- *What makes your service the best amongst your competitors?*
- *What's your cost per recruitment?*

She was shocked as he wasn't prepared for these questions and gave me some vague answers. I was waiting for her to check some data on her laptop and give me some approximate figures. She had some answers which she was unsure of as there wasn't any data to back it.

I decided to ask her some more questions:

- *How many proposals were sent in the last six months?*
- *How many were accepted?*
- *What was the average proposed pricing?*
- *What was the average accepted pricing?*
- *How many meetings did you attend?*
- *How many new clients did you approach?*
- *How many asked you to send emails?*
- *How many cold calls did you make?*
- *From where do you get your database?*
- *Percentage-wise, how much is useful data?*

These questions were making her uneasy. I observed that she had made no efforts to track the company's progress. After a while, she was, finally able to provide me with some data based on which I helped her with some calculations.

Her average earning per candidate was INR 20,000. She had done less than 100 recruitments last year. To achieve the goal of INR 10 Million, she would need to make 500 recruitments in one year. Now, this is beside the fact that we had not considered the cost for sourcing talent and clients.

The number looks steep but isn't lousy forecasting, only if we plan and have the right ingredients to make this possible.

She was unaware of competitor offering and their price points. To be in a business and not to be aware of the competition is a deadly mistake. She had not maintained any data, which meant that she had never tracked his progress.

That is when I introduced her to Sales Flow. If you ask people in the sales profession where does their sales cycle begins, the majority of them would say Approaching The Customer, which is a reactive way to the Sales process. If you consider Retail Sales, where you are an in-store salesperson, then you may carry some weight when you mention Approaching. In that scenario, the store placement, local marketing, and the products on display are used to source the right kind of customers in your store.

When you look at a B2B Sales Model, you would want to identify who the buyers are and then plan things accordingly. Hence the B2B sales cycle begins at Research.

The 'Red Snapper' Approach

Imagine someone says: *"If you have to catch a Red Snapper fish for lunch, how would you do that?"*

Hopefully, you wouldn't say something like *"I will reel in the fishing line when the Red Snapper is at the hook."*

Why? Because your process of catching a fish does not start there as you need to do a few things before you reel in the fish. So what would you do? The best strategy to adopt is to be a layman in your approach.

You may start by finding answers to questions such as:

- *How does a Red Snapper look?*
- *Where can I find Red Snappers? Is it safe to go there?*
- *How far is the place?*
- *Is it worthwhile in terms of time, the money and effort to reach there?*
- *What mode of transportation should I use?*
- *Are they found in shallow waters or deep waters? Do I need a boat to get there?*
- *What resources would I require?*
- *What is the size and weight of Red Snappers?*
- *What kind of fishing equipment do I need?*
- *What type of bait should be used to catch Red Snappers?*
- *Which is the preferred time for catching Red Snappers?*
- *Would there be a lot of people fishing for Red Snappers?*
- *Do I have the necessary information from local people?*

- *Do I have the required equipment to keep the fish fresh till I reach home?*
- *Who would cook it? What ingredients and resources are needed for cooking?*

In many ways, Selling resembles Fishing. It is more about trawling for new customers in the deep waters. People generally start with a few questions and go with the thought process that they will figure it on the way. They do not think through each aspect, and this approach may lead to a positive outcome sometimes, but it is not something that will guarantee success consistently.

A 'research-less' approach may be employed by people who want to catch the red snapper as a hobby. There are no negative consequences if they are unable to catch any. This kind of a 'we will figure it out on the way' approach with no research or planning can prove to be disastrous for sales focussed organizations.

It is imperative to plan well in advance, and the steps should be mapped out.

What Questions Should You Ask?

1. What would be the profile of your customer- How do Red Snappers look? Are they found in shallow waters or deep waters- In case of Individuals: Age Bracket, Gender, Profession, Income group, Interests, Designation, Nationality, Marital Status, Possessions such as House/Car, etc. Incase of Organizations:

Turnover, Age, Industry, Number of Employees, Sector, Location etc.

2. Where will you find the customer? In which waters can I find Red Snapper- in the physical world or the digital world?

3. Business Research, SWOT, STEEPLED Analysis- Is it safe to go there? It is essential to see if the market conditions support your product growth. It also gives you enough information for creating a Plan B and caters to 'what if' scenarios.

4. What is the Time, Money and Effort needed to market? How far is the place? ? Is it worthwhile in terms of time, the money spent and the efforts made, to reach there? It is vital to know the speed at which you can reach out to your target customers and the amount of work needed to get there.

5. What strategies must I employ? Each model has its pros and cons and the expense associated with it. Should I hire a physical workforce? Should I work on a franchisee model? Should I set up a regional office? Would a website suffice? What mode of transportation would I require? What would be the profile of the customers? What is the size and weight of Red Snappers? What kind of fishing equipment would I need?

(The first aspect refers to acquisition. The second is, matching customer expectations according to their profiles.) To meet customer requirements, the organization will have to invest in better systems and have skilled staff.

6. How to attract customers? What bait attracts Red Snappers? What Dangers or Danglers need to be highlighted for attracting customers to our product or service?

7. What is the preferred time for spotting Red Snappers? This is related to marketing and advertising. After analysing the market conditions, the products need to be positioned.

8. What about the competition? Will other people be fishing in the same waters? A knowledge of this aspect is essential as the marketing strategy and pricing need to be designed in accordance.

9. Market Research – Do I have information from the local people? This means that you want to check the acceptance of the product or product benefits before the launch. You want to understand how people would react to the product. You also need to form focus groups to help you customize the product for the local segment.

10. After Sales Support – Who would cook it, and what ingredients and resources are required for cooking? How will the Operations team take care of the customer?

Selling is similar to fishing. So do I have the required fishing skills? If you are doing it for fun, then it is not so important, but as a profession, it is essential.

The Fishing-Sales Analogy

Before you get ready for your appointment with your prospect/customer or make that phone call, make you sure you know your 'fish' well.

Do they fit into the customer profile that you are seeking? Do they match your revenue expectations? Will you be able to provide them with quality service? How and where will you be able to locate them? What will be your methods of approaching them (phone calls, messages, email, a meeting face to face)? What solutions will you offer? What problems are you going to solve?

Acquiring a customer has a high cost associated with it. It starts with the idea that gave birth to the product, followed by taking it into the market. This requires advertising, systems and backend support and that itself is a significant expense. However, catering to existing customers reduces such expenditure.

A recent study conducted showed that it costs 6-7 times more to acquire a new customer than to keep an existing one. Hence there should be an excellent team that caters to the customers and focuses on relationship building after the product is sold. A great sale is the product of effort and commitment. The right method, tools, and expertise can enable a sales organization to become a well-oiled machine that meets and exceeds sales targets every year.

Why Do We Need A Sales Cycle?

Let us take a look at the Sales Cycle and Ratios. This will give you a Guesstimate (Guess + Estimate) of what would be required from your side to achieve the sales target. There are many factors that one needs to be aware of and to optimize for success. This includes recognizing how brand image, product reviews, and marketing affect the sales cycle.

Meeting sales goals starts with a simple step. You need a target to achieve. What gets measured can be improved. Closing needs to have a number to it – in terms of the Number of Sales and the Amount Generated. These are the target figures which will be derived from your Yearly Target.

The Average Sales Price is derived by the formula (Revenue through Sales/Number of Sales).

Closing	Quarter 1	Quarter 2	Quarter 3	Quarter 4
Number Of Sales (A)				
Revenue Though Sales (B)				
Average Sales Price (C)				

The Average Sales Price (C) will be beneficial for forecasting. Assume that you would require 105 Sales for Q1 (A) to meet your revenue target, which may seem an 'easy to

Impossible Sales

achieve' figure. If we consider 90 days in Q1, it averages just more than one sale per day. Have you thought of 'How many Negotiation stages you would need to enter in?'

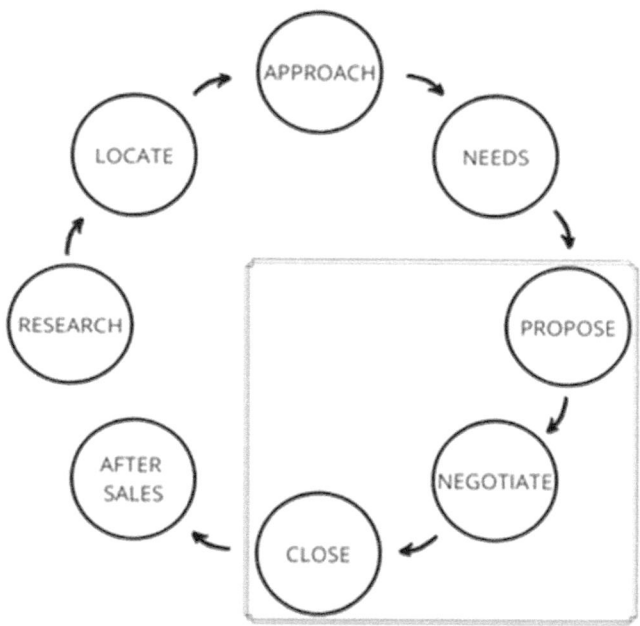

Not all the negotiations that you enter in will have a favourable outcome and result in a sale. So this figure would depend entirely on your effectiveness as a Negotiator and the efforts put in during the planning stage before entering the negotiation.

For reaching the Negotiation stage, the submitted proposal needs to be accepted. The success of this stage will depend on how effective was your 'Need Identification' and 'How effectively was the Proposal drafted'.

How Does A Sales Cycle Help You?

The Pyramid would look something similar to the figure below.

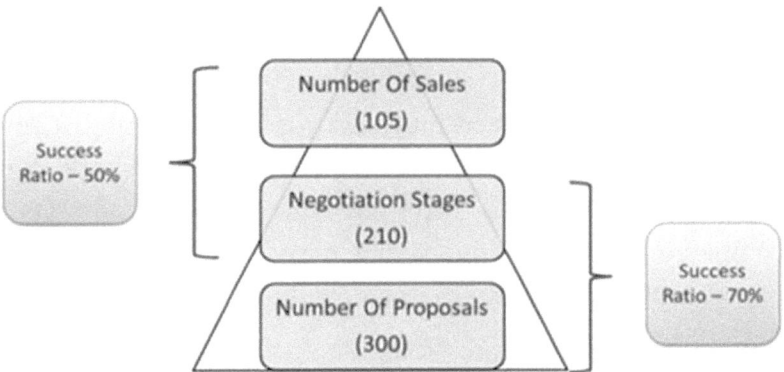

The Closing Pyramid

This is a sample indicator of how many proposals need to be submitted for getting the desired number of closes.

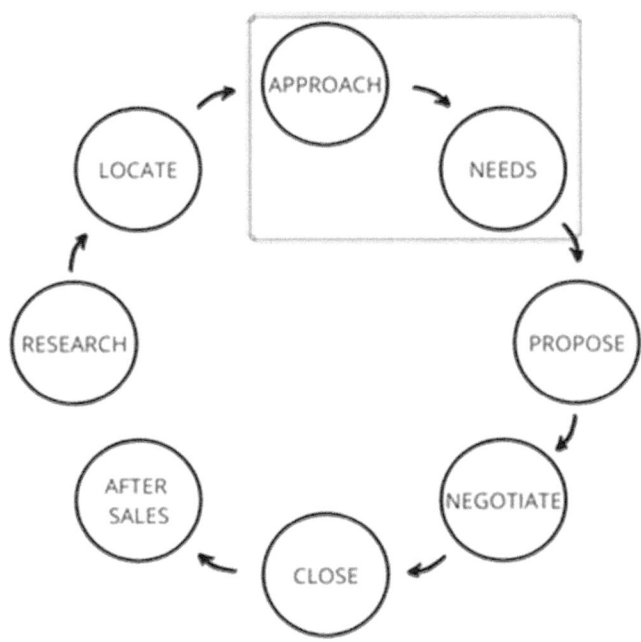

Impossible Sales

How do we get to the stage of submitting proposals?

This requires Approaching Customers, Having meetings, Identifying Needs. Not all customers that you approach would be interested in your product or service.

Those who are interested may call you for a meeting. They may get to know about your offering and check the competitor offering as well. Then they may opt for your competitor instead of you, or they may not go ahead because of some internal challenges or budget hurdles.

Creating best 'First Impressions' are very crucial in this stage.

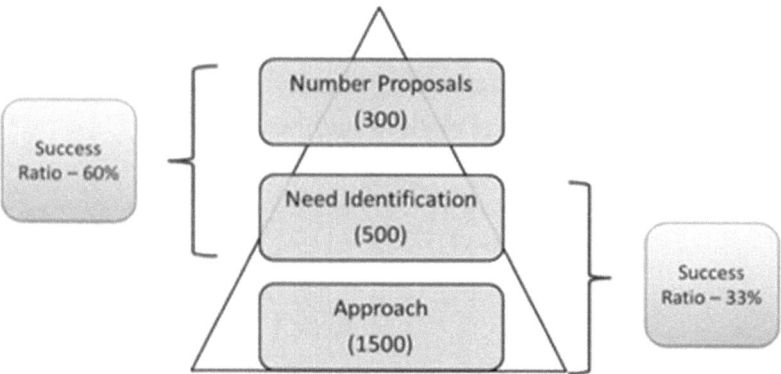

The Approach Pyramid

Well, the picture gets clear in the above scenario. With the current effectiveness, you would need 1500 Approaches to get 105 Sales which are required for meeting your target for Q1. Now the situation is getting into perspective.

How do you get to approach 1500 customers every quarter?

This brings us to the next stage of planning – Research and Locate.

How Does A Sales Cycle Help You?

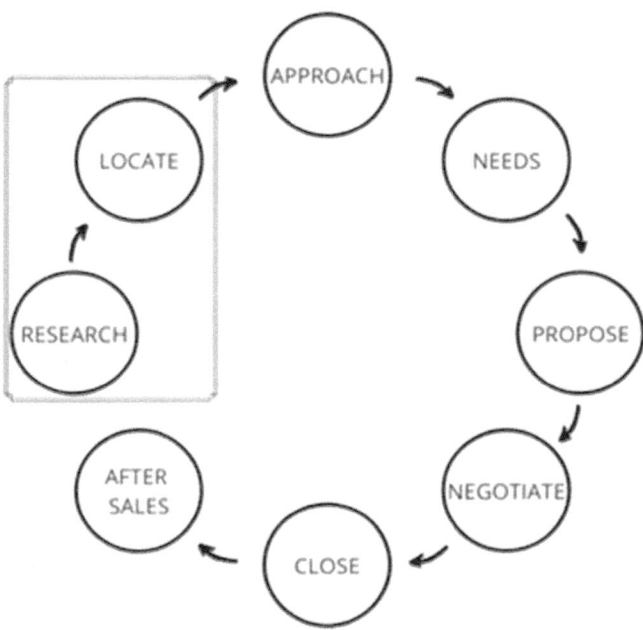

One of the biggest challenges which Sales Professionals face is reaching the right kind of audience. Remember the Red Snapper Approach – If you can profile your target customers, then the Approach Pyramid will be easier to manage.

From a customer point of view, there is a process through which they will want to interact with you. This is called the Brand Radar.

The Brand Radar

How do you reach out to more customers? There are many ways apart from corporate marketing – which an organization uses to create brand awareness.

Impossible Sales

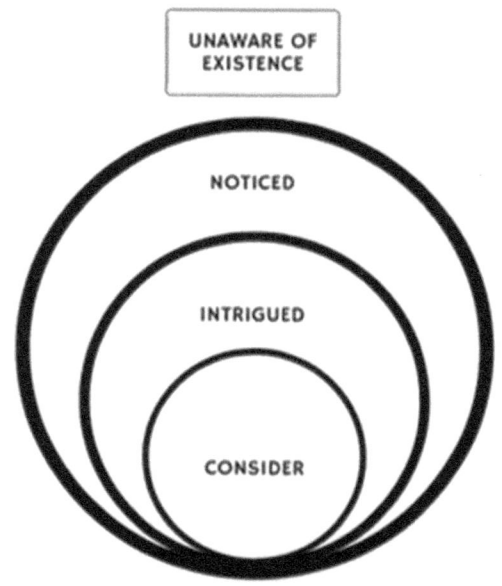

Let's look at the steps to be positioned in the brand radar.

Benefits Of A Robust Brand Radar

Think about these specific moments. As a child, when you fell and grazed your knee, you asked for a Band-Aid, not a bandage. As a college student or a professional, you needed a Xerox copy, not a photocopy. When you wanted a drink at a fast-food restaurant, you asked for a Coke, not a carbonated beverage.

How Do Customers Interact With Companies?

In the first place, customers are unaware of the product's existence. Next, they notice a product or service, and they are intrigued and wish to explore it in detail. They consider buying the product and then take the plunge. The Steps 'Noticed', 'Intrigued' and 'Consider' will get you closer to the customer, and that's when the product offering is shared. Advertising or Cold Canvassing (Sales Professionals approaching potential clients through emails or calls or visits) can create Brand Awareness, and people may start taking notice of the product. Displaying USPs (Unique Selling Points) will get the customers 'Intrigued', and they would be willing to consider. If at this stage, the approach happens, the chances of conversion increase exponentially.

We need to take a new approach to comprehend the customer's journey. We need to rethink our strategies and assist customers/prospects as they go through this cycle.

In this digital age, companies have a variety of resources to share their message across media platforms. They can use social media to connect directly with customers, get fans to become amateur brand ambassadors, and connect with the customers by addressing customer concerns in exhibitions, webinars, and others to build a unique and robust reputation.

The easiest way of distinguishing yourself from your competitors is to find out what they have in common and then find what the value addition you can have. Your guiding principle here will be to lead and never follow. Find your differentiators and create a niche for yourself in the market. Customers will always remember you as the one with the unique selling point. Dazzle them with something they have never thought, seen or heard before. For example, people have struggled for years to get the ketchup (in a steady flow)

Impossible Sales

out of the bottle, shaking it, pounding the bottle on the counter, trying every trick in the book. That's when Heinz had an 'aha' moment and decided to turn its ketchup bottles upside down. Heinz created magic with a unique idea and gravity.

The Sales professional also needs to position the brand and product to the customer segments which have been identified. An increased number of customers reached will have better brand awareness as well as 'Intrigues'. Brand Awareness will help you to get noticed. It may not help you get more sales immediately; however, it will help you in creating sustainability of presence, which can then result in Intrigues.

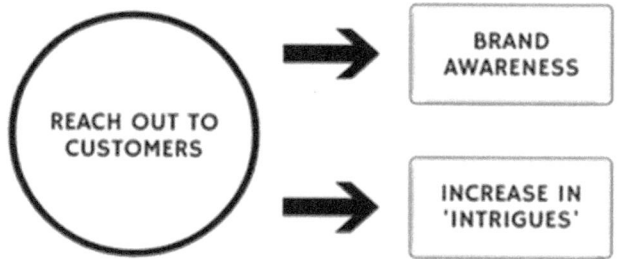

How do you (an individual) reach out to more customers?

- Emails
- Phone Calls
- Physical Visits
- Fax
- Hardcopy Mailers
- Newspaper Inserts

- Digital Footprint
- Social Media Advertising
- Presence In related groups (Physical or Digital)
- References
- Messaging Platforms
- Location-Based Marketing
- Print Media
- Promotion during events
- Collaborations with other brands
- Tie-ups with organizations
- Roadshows
- Independent Promoters
- _____
- _____

The more ways you have, to reach out, the stronger your presence would be. Here the success ratio would completely depend on the appeal of the brand, product positioning and the attractiveness of the marketing campaign. What needs to be worked on here is the 'Intrigue' factor.

This is similar to a shop display in a mall. If you like something about the display products (quality, price, colour, fit, offer, etc.), you may tend to walk into the shop. However, you may not purchase the same thing on display as you would be welcomed with many choices. Your mailers, inserts, digital footprint needs to act as a shop display – to captivate customers!

For doing all this, there needs to be a lot of time spent in research – first deciding the goal, then designing the strategy and lastly, implementing that strategy.

The Most Underrated Element – After Sales

In a successful sales cycle, this seemingly the last part, however the most critical element too. One of the mistakes which mediocre sales professionals do is treat this very lightly. They feel that once the sale is closed, their job is done. Professional salespeople know that they can still get more sales if they nourish the relationship.

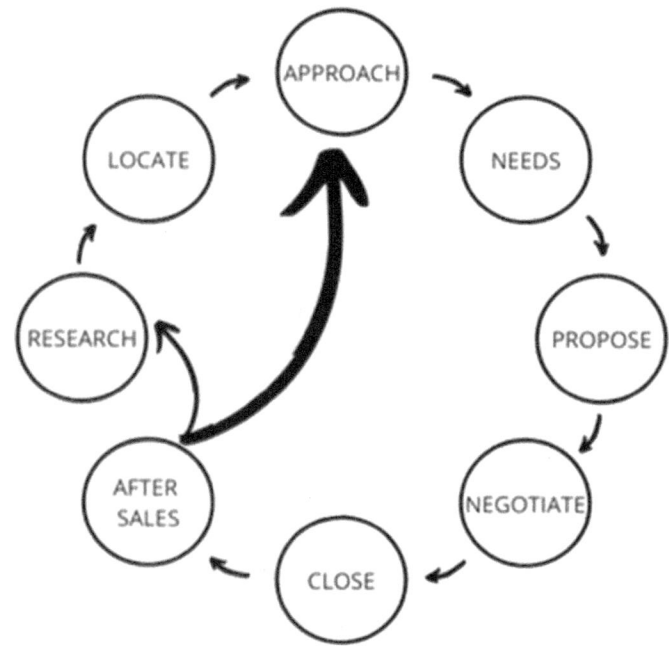

Some unstated rules in this element:

Ask For Referrals After The Sale Is Done

This is usually the best time to ask for referrals as the customers are elated with the purchase. If your negotiation has been spot-on, the customers will feel that they have got a fantastic deal, and most of them would want their near and dear ones to benefit too. Most salespeople either forget asking for referrals, or they feel that it's not appropriate. Remember, there is no harm in asking. The best answer is 'Yes', and the worst response is 'No'. This is a position where you have nothing to lose and everything to gain.

Reach Out Within 7 Days Or 15 Days Of The Sale

It is good to check if everything is ok and if the customer is happy. If there are any issues, it allows you to sort things. This step can go a long way in building a dense relationship. Customers feel that you care and will be there for them. This gives you an additional opportunity to build rapport.

Get Feedback About The Sales Cycle

Getting an honest feedback can help you improvise your offering to other customers.

Make The Sales Cycle Work

If you want a 100% change, instead of changing 1 thing by 100%, change 100 things by 1%, which is much easier. In the Sales cycle, changing the approach and execution in each stage can drastically affect the outcome.

[ACTION POINTS]

Research
Be ahead of the curve and move with the technology. Use Artificial Intelligence-based tools to determine where your product or service will be more valued and respected.

Locate
Find relevant customers using Social Media and Digital Marketing tools. Visit events where your target customers are spending time (in Physical as well as Digital World). Use the traditional methods of Cold Calling, Visiting and Advertising wisely.

Approach
Figure out the best way to approach your potential customers. Would it be through Email or Phone Call or Personal Visit? Once you connect, get them added on Social Media. Create scripts that have a benefit statement as an Attention Grabber, and the body is infused with NLP Elements. In case it is done on a call, match the pace and keywords used. Make your first impression a memorable one.

Needs

Take a product from the portfolio, identify the features and advantages and narrow down to problems which can be solved. Have a questioning sequence designed for the customers to understand the impact of the Danger and Dangler.

Propose

Once you have at least three needs identified, then would be an ideal time to propose your product as a solution. Here an NLP element of mirroring and matching is used, where you mirror the body language of the customer to establish subconscious rapport.

Negotiate

Prior planning can maximize profits. Think what will be your:

Walk Away Point – The price below which you won't be able to go

Maximum Expected – This is the price you would ideally want

Anchor – this is the first price to be put on the table and should ideally be 10% more than your Maximum Expected.

Variables – Apart from Price, what other elements will affect the negotiation? Rate them based on the 'Cost To You' and 'Value For Customer'.

Once you have identified these, then anticipate these from customer's position. What do you think would be their 'Walk Away', 'Maximum Expected', 'Anchor' and 'Variables'.

Having this information will put you in a better position to negotiate.

Close

This is the most crucial stage as all the efforts boil down to closing the sale. One of the well-kept secrets of top sales professionals is checking if the rapport is established, and then proposing the solution.

Through the interaction, the sales professional matches the body language and then changes his or her body language to see if the customer does the same. If yes, that means the rapport is strong, and it is the ideal time to ask for the close.

Of the many closing techniques, the following are more effective:

Direct Close: Asking for the sale directly. i.e. "Shall we go ahead with it?" or "Would you like me to book your order?"

Alternate Choice Close: Giving 2 or 3 choices, assuming that the customer has said yes. i.e. "Would you purchase by cash

> *Mastering every element requires practice*

or card?" or "When would you like the delivery, this week or next week?"

Fear Close: People don't like to miss something good. So installing a fear that they might lose on something can work well if it is genuine. i.e. "The offer may not be valid the next week." or "The discounted price will not be there tomorrow."

After-Sale

Ask for referrals. Check with them after a week or 15 days if everything is alright. If there are any issues, solve it on priority. Find ways to build relationships. When you connect, don't always ask for business.

7 How To Set Achievable Goals?

How to make them efficient and effective?

Planning For Time Management

So far, whenever we have talked about planning, we have looked at the numbers and ratios. But there is another crucial aspect that brings all these strategies to fruition, and that is the first step – Planning for Time Management.

"He who every morning plans the transaction of the day and follows out that plan, carries a thread that will guide him through the maze of the most busy life. But where no plan is laid, where the disposal of time is surrendered merely to the chance of incidence, chaos will soon reign."

– Victor Hugo

What Is Time Management?

Irrespective of how popular the term is, one can't Manage Time; you can only Manage Yourself With Respect To Time. Time Management refers to the way we organize, prioritize, and allocate time for specific activities. Effective time management leads to better efficiency, enhanced productivity, less stress, work-life balance, and excellent opportunities for professional and personal growth.

Similarly, each activity in the Sales Cycle requires a certain amount of time to perfect it. Hence, managing self with respect to time becomes critical.

We move to the second step. We hear people talking about a Vision and a Goal. What is the difference between the two? Vision is to see and imagine a future with purpose-driven goals. Goals turn your vision into reality by working on your objectives with a plan.

As a sales professional, you may have a vision of being the Top Sales Professional in your team or your organization. This cannot be achieved by saying *"I want it to happen"* and expect it to happen on its own; you need to define your goals.

Most sales professionals or managers target short-term goals. They seek results daily with no planning for the future. To maximize profits, they must work on a long- term vision. A clear goal helps to prioritize and organize activities accordingly. Goals are a series of measurable activities that assist you in fulfilling your vision. Goals will help you outline and measure the milestones crossed in the journey towards your vision. Some goals are decided for us by the organizations we work for, and some we set for ourselves. All these goals require meticulous planning for them to materialize. You need to picture what you want to achieve. That is why it is called a Vision.

What is your Vision, and how do you determine Goals?

Start by asking yourself these questions:

- What do you want to achieve in your personal life?
- Why do you want to achieve it?.
- How are you going to handle any setbacks?

Once you have identified the personal goals, you are ready to set your professional goals.

- What are your professional goals?
- Have you refined them into stage-wise targets?
- How will it impact your personal life?
- Do you have a plan in mind for achieving your goals?
- What will you do to augment your skill sets?

Once you have answers to these questions, you need to prepare a course of action to fulfill your vision.

- What will you do to attain your goals?
- What tools/skills do you need to achieve them?

How To Set Achievable Goals?

S.M.A.R.T.E.S.T. Goals

Various factors influence our decisions while setting goals. The diagram above displays professional, business, family, financial, health, personal, and religious/inspirational angles. In each of the areas, we must set multiple goals. Once these goals are set, they need to be shaped expertly. That's where S.M.A.R.T.E.S.T goals come into the picture (the earlier acronym S.M.A.R.T. is now refined to S.M.A.R.T.E.S.T.)

Specific – What is the precise goal?

Measurable – How do we track the milestones achieved? How do we know when we have reached our goal?

Attainable – Can it be achieved?

Realistic – Can I achieve it?

Time Bound – By when should the goal be achieved?

Exciting – If any setbacks are experienced, the excitement of achieving the goal fuels the motivation

Significant – Why do you care about achieving the goal?

Toward – Moving toward the state you want to reach

How would you position the statement 'I want as many customers as possible' in the S.M.A.R.T.E.S.T format?

Specific – From Dubai, Hotel Industry, Company Turnover more than USD 2 Million

Measurable – 1050 Customers in the year with an average sale value of $2000

Achievable – By taking into account the factors such as Manpower, Money, Machinery, Methods, Materials, Milieu, Measurement, Maintenance and Management

Realistic – By increasing the marketing spend for brand awareness, Hiring 2 Sales Professionals. Time-Bound – By financial year closing (31st March 2021)

Exciting – What are the rewards it would give, i.e., Incentives, reputation boost, Promotion, etc.

Significant – How will it help you to achieve your professional goal of being the top salesperson? What will be the level of achievement?

Toward – Is it a goal that will help you achieve other bigger goals professionally or personally?

Goal setting can take time. You must think through the process well. To make sure that you are successful in achieving each of your goals, it is necessary to also take into account the what-if scenarios.

The Pareto Principle

The Pareto principle, the rule of vital few and trivial many, was named after Vilfredo Pareto, an Italian economist. He noticed that 20% of the Italian population owned 80% of Italy's wealth. He also realized that only 20% of the pea pods in his garden produced 80% of his pea crop each year. He figured that this 80-20 principle could be adapted to almost anything in the world.

In business, Pareto Principle can help us to determine:

- Customers responsible for the bulk of your revenue
- Issues liable for the majority of your problems.
- Factors affecting your numbers

In your life, this principle will help you to understand:

- Things, experiences, and people that bring you happiness
- What are the top things which can bring professional success

So, the Pareto Principle shows us that:

- A small number of causes are responsible for a large percentage of the effect-usually a 20-percent to 80-percent ratio.
- This ratio applies to almost anything in the world, from management to personal life to natural phenomena.
- Focusing on 20% of the most problematic issues will clear up 80% of it.

The Pareto Principle – where does it figure in goal setting? The 80:20 Rule. As per this rule, 80% of the time, things will go as planned. There are chances that you will face hurdles or obstacles in the remaining 20%.

You could take this 20% as your extra cushion. Instead of having a target of 100, keep an increased target, or allow for some buffer time while keeping an end date. This added cushion will safeguard you against unexpected challenges.

Whenever any unexpected incident occurs, you will have the resources to tackle it. This makes you less stressful because you know that you will still be able to reach your goal.

[TIME FOR ACTION]

Keeping the above points in mind, take some time and identify 5 priorities and then create your S.M.A.R.T.E.S.T goals.

The Influence Of Positive Words And Thinking

It is essential to use the present tense while setting your Goal Statements. Statements like 'I am earning $5000 as incentives....' appeal more to the subconscious mind. By writing your goals in the present tense, you are feeding your brain great motivating visuals. The use of positive words while setting goals is encouraged. Instead of saying what you will NOT do, write down what you are going to do in the form of positive statements.

To understand the effect of positive words, refer to Dr.Masaru Emoto's research in which he studied the impact of different words on water crystals. Dr. Emoto captured water's expressions. He developed a technique using a powerful microscope in a cold room and used high-speed photography to capture newly formed crystals of frozen water samples. Dr. Emoto discovered that crystals formed in frozen water reveal changes when specific, concentrated thoughts are directed toward them. He found that water from clear springs and water that has been exposed to loving words showed brilliant, intricate, and colorful snowflake patterns. In contrast, polluted water, or water exposed to negative thoughts, forms incomplete, asymmetrical patterns with dull colors.

It shouldn't come as a surprise that many religions also have a holy water concept, signifying that our ancestors knew about it.

Many tests have proven that if plants are spoken to lovingly, they grow well and bear sweeter fruits and have a lovely blossom. Kinesiology experiments performed on people demonstrate the power of positive thinking affecting the belief system, and upto 60% of the human adult body is water.

Just setting goals may not help you to achieve it. The conscious brain may have helped you set goals, but there is another driver, which is more powerful – your subconscious mind. Some say that the subconscious mind is 6000 times more powerful than the conscious mind. Some say that it is a million times more powerful. There is no proof of measurement, and these elements are metaphysical. Just as we know that the universe is vast and unexplained, the subconscious is immensely powerful. Many successful people attribute their success to effectively harnessing the power of the subconscious mind.

By learning to master your mind, you can produce some amazingly effective results that you have been working for in your life. The mind determines your belief and your success. The subconscious mind is in charge of almost everything in your life, especially your mental and emotional processes. The subconscious mind has the answer to all of the issues and challenges you have been facing. Your subconscious mind can propel you to achieve the goals that you have dreamed of.

Make sure you keep repeating your goals and objectives (to yourself) positively all the time. Repetition makes the subconscious mind seize the desire/goal at hand and store it. The subconscious mind is also very attentive to your talents and skills. Engage regularly with your abilities, and the subconscious mind will help to apply it whenever the need arises. Listen to your inner mind as the subconscious mind corresponds with us through our emotions, feelings, and intentions. Our subconscious mind leads us to opportunities or leads us away from disasters. Broaden your mind by considering new lines of thinking.

Breakaway from what was holding you back in the past. To achieve your goals, reach for your dreams, take yourself out of your comfort zone, and work on your plan of action. Change your life, identify what you want, set them down on paper. Be as clear and precise about what it is that you want because your goals must be as explicit as possible. Channel all your energy towards your goal. Write down to the last detail- what you want- and then, you will need to imagine that you have already received it. Be passionate about your goal and commit time and energy to think about how you can make it possible.

How To Make The Subconscious Mind Work For You?

3 Steps For Goal Achievements

1) Create Visuals

If your goal is to be a top sales professional, then think of yourself as one. How would you look like the top salesperson? Imagine how you would look when you are receiving the award? Now create a visual. Search for a photo of someone getting an award of the top Sales Person. Replace the award winner's face with your face. Get the image printed and put it on a Vision Board. I recommend reading the book 'The Secret' by Rhonda Byrne.

2) Use Affirmations

Affirmations are sentences such as 'Money Flows To Me Easily And Effortlessly' (Recommended Reading – The Power Is Within You by Louise Hay). Once you have written these statements, record them and listen to them when just before sleeping and when you are waking up. That's the time when our subconscious is active, and consciously we can do something to program it.

3) *Surround Yourself With The Visuals And Affirmations*

When the goals are ambitious, one needs to be comfortable with the idea. Your mind sees the visuals often, and then it starts believing in the visuals and paves the way for creating that reality.

For some of you, this may sound strange as it does not appeal to the logical mind; however, it works.

Have you, as a kid, tried magnetizing a piece of iron? We had an experiment in our Physics book – if you wrap wire on an iron nail and connect both ends to the battery, (Like the figure), the Iron nail turns into a magnet till the time the electricity is passing through it. A small piece of iron that can't lift a feather on its own can lift heavier metal pieces when magnetized.

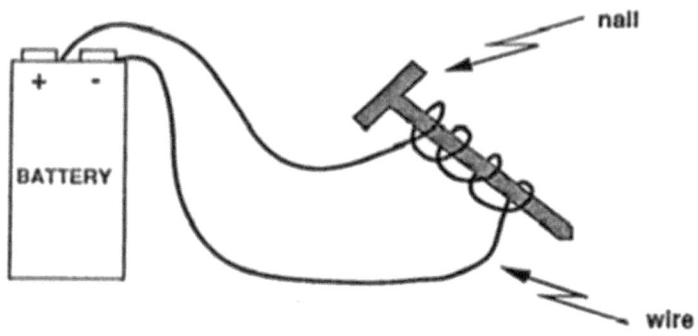

The same principle applies to the goals. When the coil of belief encompasses the goals, it gets powered by the subconscious mind, and there are innumerable possibilities drawn into existence.

A study showed that people who were training their biceps only in their mind, increased their muscles by 15 %, while the other group who went to the gym for real training, increased the muscles by 30 %. So pure mental training is almost as effective as an actual workout.

Having focussed thoughts, and feeding the subconscious with them, increases the intensity and aids in bringing the goal closer in reality.

Many athletes and sports enthusiasts use mental rehearsal. Focused intention and visualization have proved to change and improve physical performance. Mental rehearsal is when you pre-think and pre-feel the situation as if it was real. The most important thing here is to include all your senses and think as if it was real and already happening. Research has shown that the electrical activity in the brain is the same, whether we are only thinking about it or doing it. So when you continuously feed your mind with the goal statements, affirmations, and visualization, the goal will manifest in your real life.

Now comes the tricky part – In one of the experiments conducted, it was found out that there are 15,000-70,000 thoughts which come to a human mind in a day. Yes – in a day!

So we need to make sure that consciously we need to restrict the distracting thoughts and focus on those aligned to our goals and objectives.

One of the things we can do consciously is managing and prioritizing the activities so that we always focus on getting the maximum done. Excellent time management means being effective, as well as efficient. In the modern, fast-paced workplace, it can be hard to distinguish between what's important and urgent. We often fall in the trap of believing all urgent tasks are also important, even if that's seldom the case. Most of the things trying to get our brain's attention are usually trivial, non-important tasks, with a high sense of urgency.

One of the best ways is using the Eisenhower Method (well known as the Urgent and Important matrix). The Eisenhower Matrix was advanced by Dwight D. Eisenhower, the 34th President of the United States. He also served as a General in the United States Army and as the Allied Forces Supreme Commander during World War II. The Eisenhower Matrix is a simple yet powerful model for categorizing tasks according to their urgency and importance.

THE EISENHOWER MATRIX

	URGENT	NOT URGENT
IMPORTANT	**DO** IT NOW	**DECIDE** TO SCHEDULE A TIME TO DO IT
NOT IMPORTANT	**DELEGATE** IT TO SOMEONE ELSE	**DELETE** IT NOW

This Eisenhower matrix has four quadrants with different plans of action which help to determine the urgency of one's tasks: do (urgent and important), schedule (not urgent but important), delegate (urgent but not important), and delete/eliminate/reduce (neither urgent nor important). By deciding whether a task belongs in one of these quadrants, it is easy to prioritize, schedule, or delegate it.

Time is the most valuable thing a man can spend.

– Theophrastus

Most successful Sales Professionals use this model to manage their time. Each task and activity, which is essential for you to reach your goal, should be categorized into the Eisenhower Matrix. This would also include the activities in your personal life. When one wants to achieve goals, one should look at every aspect. And, then, act on your plan right away.

Time is invaluable because it cannot be bought, and hence it is crucial to managing ourselves in time we have wisely. Erroneous time management leads to stress and burnout. The ability to categorize our priorities effectively will increase efficiency and lead to a successful life.

8 How To Double Positive Attitude?

How to make it a way of life?

Breaking The 4-Minute Mile Barrier

"It stood there as something that was waiting to be done, and I was in the right place at the right time and was ready to do it. My attitude was that it can be done, and it will be done soon, and I'd rather it were done here."
- Roger Bannister

"If you want something you've never had, you must be willing to do something you've never done."

– Thomas Jefferson

On May 6, 1954, Roger Bannister became the first person in documented history to break the record of the 4-Minute Mile. Roger Bannister, a medical student at the University of Oxford, was studying to be a neurologist, and running was a spare-time passion. Those days, running a 4-minute mile was considered to be an unconquerable, unachievable feat. Bannister never followed accepted training methods and devised his training techniques. Hence, the term- the Lone Wolf Miler. And so, too, on that day at Oxford, he ran the last turns on the track by himself.

The four-minute mile was an elusive target for many runners. It was a challenge that many runners felt could not be won. Bannister showed that the four-minute mile was an achievable goal, and the physical and psychological barriers can be overcome. Forty-six days later, John Landy, an Australian runner, conquered the mile in just 3 minutes and 58 seconds. Barely a year later, three runners broke the four-minute obstacle in a single race. More than a thousand runners have crossed the 4-minute mile since then.

Roger Bannister made the impossible, possible. He crashed the psychological barriers to achievement and demonstrated that if there is a will, there is a way. Hicham El Guerrouj holds the current record of 3:43.13.

On October 12, 2019, Eluid Kipchoge accomplished a feat that's akin to scaling Mt. Everest for the first time. The 34-year-old Kenyan man ran the fastest 26.2 miles ever by clocking in at 1:59:40 on a course in Vienna. This made him the first person to ever run a marathon distance in under two hours. Just to break that down, it means he ran each mile in under four minutes and 34 seconds a staggering 26 times in a row.

You might wonder what does the 4-Minute Mile or a Marathon has to have to do with Sales.

Well, the logic remains the same. What was once considered unattainable, is in your grasp now. This example shows us that in any field of work or study, we need to break away from conventional ways of thinking that limit our progress. Do things that you have never done before, and that will make all the difference. If someone can achieve it, so can you. It's possible and achievable. And you, too, can create records!

Desire Needs Action (Dna)

For achieving challenging goals, certain prerequisites are essential:

- A stubborn heart
- An intense desire to succeed
- The ability to adapt to change
- Hard work
- The knowledge and skill to do it!

The very fact that you are reading this book signifies that you do have a desire to succeed. Stubbornness, intensity, adaptability, and hard work cannot be compensated. Knowing how to do it, that's what this book is for. This book shows you the ropes to breaking your 4-Minute Mile.

Though this chapter has been placed towards the end of the book, it is the most crucial element in your race towards success. A positive mental attitude is a vital factor, without which desired success will only remain an elusive aspiration.

Let's take the 31st December scenario. Many of you will be able to relate it. December 31 is the day when many people make resolutions – New Year Resolutions. One of the most common resolutions is about image building, the desire to have a toned body, or a desirable body. On the way to a new year party, an advertisement flashes in front of you – gym membership for one year at a whopping 60% off. The deal appears to be too good to resist, and you take the gym membership. There are numerous trips to the store in search of the perfect gym clothes and shoes. The excitement builds.

Your friends have advised you that the best time to exercise is in the morning. So you schedule your gym hours in the morning. Let us see what happens next:

Day 1

You keep an alarm for 6 am. You are excited as you are willing and prepared to start something new. You want to challenge yourself to do your best as you know that in today's fast-paced environment, your time is precious. You have realized that you have prioritized your health and well being after work and family, but that is not enough. You are determined and have been able to set aside time for some physical activity, and so, with your goal in mind, your head held high and a smile on your face, you set foot in the gym. You work out as instructed and come back from the gym, a couple of hours later, feeling exhausted but satisfied. It was the right decision to make! You look at yourself in the mirror, the sweat-drenched clothes look great. You consult the gym dietician who advises you to drink a protein shake every day. The next day you get the expensive protein shake powder as you have embarked on a healthy lifestyle.

Day 2

You consult the dietitian, once again, and you are provided with a specific diet that you need to consume in a timely fashion. There are some things that you need to stop eating. Well- those seem to be favorites- but you are confident that you can stay away from them. Then you go to the gym and start sweating it out again as your goal is uppermost in your mind. You will not procrastinate as you are determined and so your gym instructor welcomes you with a smile every day. You feel exhausted but charged up. When you go home, you look at yourself in the mirror, but you don't see a significant difference, yet the sweat-drenched clothes indicate that you are on the right path. You are putting in the effort as you know that Rome was not built in a day.

Day 3

The alarm rings, but you need some more sleep. So you press the snooze button, but your 15 minutes turns to 30 minutes, and you stumble out of bed. Your fitness goal is on your mind; you have not forgotten it. So you get dressed and head for the gym, but today, you have decided to exercise for a shorter period. You work out, head back home, and as usual, the sweat-drenched clothes continue to make you feel better. But there is no noticeable difference in your body. You shower, get ready, and head for work. Your colleagues order pizza at work, and you refuse. Colleagues insist that nothing will happen if you take one piece, and you still refuse. You miss those days where you enjoyed pizzas.

Day 4

The alarm rings, you hit the snooze button as you are still very sleepy. Your eyes open 15 minutes later, but your mind tells you that your body needs rest after three consecutive days at the gym, and you deserve a bit of rest. After all, you have been hitting the gym every morning for the past three days. You resolve to go the next day. You know that the delay of a day will not take you away from your goal.

Day 5

When the alarm rings, you tell yourself – today is a hectic day as there is an important meeting in the morning at the office for which you need to prepare. You also need to attend the parent-teacher conference at kid's school, and so you won't have time for the gym today. You will try to go in the evening, though. In the evening, you are so exhausted that you postpone going to the gym for the next day. Yet, you know your goal.

Day 6

The alarm rings, and as you stretch your hand to silence it, you realize that your muscles are aching. Your mind tells you that maybe it will be better to take rest today, how will you exercise if your muscles are paining. The weekend has started, and you plan to spend time with your family. Life at work has been stressful too. A setback or two will not hold you back.

Day 7

The alarm sounds and the voices in your head tell you that you can take one more day off. Since it will take time to reach your goal and you have a one-year membership, going to the gym tomorrow will be ok. Meanwhile, during the day, you also decide that you might as well have some of your favorite food today. The absence of a disciplined diet for a day will not make a significant difference.

And so it begins. Does this seem familiar? That's how the human mind works.

External motivation is not everything. Motivation must come from within. To sustain motivation, patience, and hard work are keys.

An internal/intrinsically motivated activity is attempted for the sheer joy of doing it. There is no external reward, such as money or applause. Your enthusiasm arises from within, and the completion of the activity fills you with positive emotions. At work, though productivity can be raised by external factors such as incentives and a bonus, the real motivator is internal/intrinsic. Any activity that is advantageous, worthwhile, interesting, and, most importantly, demanding drives you to come up with unique ideas and innovative solutions.

The same applies to sales. Change is mandatory.

Nothing Changes, If Nothing Changes!

In the earlier example, you decided to enroll at the gym because of a new year's resolution and a discounted gym membership fee. It was just a desire to see a better version of yourself.

Exercise is integral to weight loss and health, but it is painful if you are not someone who does it every day. The reason why the gym schedule didn't work is that pleasure was not a major motivator. Imagine a situation where you are walking on the beach. You are enjoying the beauty of your surroundings when suddenly you feel dizzy and fall unconscious. When you open your eyes, you are in a hospital bed. When you are to be discharged from the hospital, the doctor says, *"If you don't work out for an hour, at least, every day, there are chances that such instances can occur again. And the next time, the consequences will be major."*

Once you have had such a health scare the consequences shared by the doctor, things will be different. You came face to face with the reality of your situation, and you understand that exercise is the key to what you value most – your life. How will this change your thinking and priorities? Will you look for excuses to press the snooze button? Your reason has changed now, and whether rain or shine, you will make it a point to find time for exercise.

What changed was the motivator. In the first case, the motivator was a Dangler. But, now, it is Danger.

Danger is a bigger motivator than a Dangler. Hence, one of the prerequisites for success is the intense desire to succeed.

If the desire is simply a desire without an action plan or purpose, then the result will be no different from the gym example.

This understanding can be used effectively in Sales. When you are focussing on New Customers, the majority are interested in Dangler, and an Experienced Customer is approaching you, it is mostly because of a Danger they want to prevent.

In one of a stock broking company, this learning was used very effectively. A team of 150 telecallers was to convince people to open a stockbroking account and transfer an initial amount for trading or investments. Their calling base came from lead generation campaigns. Some of these prospects had no knowledge about Stockbroking while others had traded earlier, through a different stock broking company. After attending a training session, they realized that New people wanted to benefit from short term trading, or they were interested in putting aside some money every month for the long term (Dangler). Experienced prospects were looking at how can they have lesser fees or gain more profits (Danger).

Hence a customized opening was constructed for the telecallers:

"Greetings I am ABC calling from XYZ company. Congratulations! You have taken your first step towards Wealth Creation and Long Term Security. How has your experience been in the Stock Trading Market?"

The response was gauged to know if the prospect is a New or Experienced customer.

For New Customers:

"What made you reach out to us today?"

"What are your expectations, Short Term Profits, or Long Term Investments?"

(These trigger questions were then used for profiling and understanding the Dangler, before the pull-based sales pitch)

For Experienced Customers
(Who were/are with competitors):

"Considering your previous stockbroker, how would you rate their services on a scale of 1-10, where one is the lowest and ten is the highest?"

If the response is between 0-9, ask, *"What makes you not give them a 10, what were the issues?"*

If the response is 10 – *"That's nice. What makes you approach us?"*

(The trigger question was to uncover and develop the 'Danger')

Once the motive was known, then the sales pitch became much more straightforward.

That organization was averaging 1463 sales in a month, and after implementation of this opening, their average sales jumped to 1958 only in 2 months. That's how powerful this approach is.

So, is multiplying your sales possible? It is definitely possible. Is it achievable? It is. If others have done it, so can you.

What would happen if you don't make the changes now?

Possibly, life will continue in the same way. The sales figures will be stagnant or decline. But due to inflation, the cost of living will continuously increase, and that will compromise your lifestyle.

What would happen if you make the changes now?

You sell more, your work-life balance is maintained, you grow financially too. It will give you the freedom to do the things that you like to do. Take your family for a vacation to exotic places, pursue your hobbies, give back to society, have a better lifestyle, and still have no worries regarding finances.

The second option seems more practical. , then start implementing all the suggestions and multiply your sales!

The Sales Diet

The most complex organ of the human body and the most remarkable one is the brain. The Greek philosophers believed that it is also connected to the scientific unknown – the mind. People ask, "What is the difference between the brain and the mind?"

The brain can be defined easily. It is the physical bundle of neurons inside a person's head and is capable of sending chemical signals to the rest of the body. Even the simplest of animals have a brain.

Scientists have tried to create a supercomputer that can act as a brain. This supercomputer weighed more than 200 tons and was the size of two basketball fields and capable of working faster than the brain. Consider this -the average weight of our brain is 3.3 pounds. Still, it beats the supercomputer because supercomputers don't have a mind, which gives it the ability to think and create. Only the mind is capable of thought. Thoughts create an Energy Signature or Aura, which attracts what it thinks. It is like holding a sign which states 'Come to Me'. Many people have shared that their Life Experiences have shaped their thought process. Even if two people face the same situation, their thought process is never similar. We either act or react to a situation. How we chose to face any situation is decided by what our mind instructs us to do.

Take a look at this example:

Two men behind bars. One saw mud, and other saw stars.

What we have here is a difference in the way the jailbirds looked at the situation. If you have negative thoughts, you will attract negativity. Some of us say, "Well, I don't have negative thoughts. I am a positive thinker, but nothing good happens. Why?" That's where the word 'focus' comes into the picture. Imagine 70,000 thoughts entering the human mind in a day. It is said that energy flows where attention goes.

So if you want something in life, then focus is the key. No distractions. Pure focus. Then anchor your thoughts with feelings and beliefs.

You can create the life you want with your:

- Thoughts
- Words
- Desires
- Beliefs
- Intent
- Emotions
- Feelings

They have the power to place you on the beautiful road to happiness, peace of mind, and achievements. Remember, the power of your subconscious is more powerful than the power of your conscious. All that you need to do is to harness the power. You can mind your matters. Many famous dieticians have shared that having the desired body structure is 70% Right Diet and 30% Physical Exercise.

Remember:

Desire Needs Action!

A similar concept applies to Sales. Having the right mindset and having the right approach is an integral part of the sales diet – 70%. The remaining 30% is achieved by following the planned approach and designing the routine.

9 The Power Of Consistency

How to harness it for immense success?

The Hammer Story

My first job in the corporate world was that of a Tele-Sales Representative in a contact center. I was selected as a member of a project that sold credit cards with a low credit limit and a high-interest rate (APR-Annual Percentage Rate). This was the first project of that contact center, and the project went live after a long wait of 1 month. I remember making a sale on the first day, and this achievement was acknowledged and celebrated by the management. I made three sales in four hours, which

"It's not what we do once in a while that shapes our lives. It's what we do consistently."

– Anthony Robbins

indicated that I had got the hang of the sales process, and from that day on, I started making consistent sales. My targets increased, and I loved the challenge as I knew I would be able to achieve them with no extra effort. I was known as 'Mr.Dependable'. The Quality Team, which monitored sales calls, stopped listening to my sales pitches because my calls adhered to guidelines and were of the highest quality. I was awarded a certificate for the best performance, and then I was given the task of handling demanding customers, guiding peers, and training new people.

The organization was growing, and very soon, I knew they would require more employees, including Team Leaders. One day, they announced six Internal Job Postings (IJP). My joy knew no bounds. I was so excited and thought that this is my next step. The interview went well, and I was elated. For the next couple of days, I pretended I was a Team Leader and started behaving like one. Who would not entertain thoughts like that – I mean, I was Mr. Dependable, consistent performer, high-quality calls, helping others achieve targets, handling demanding customers, and training new employees. A person, like me, who was committed and extremely dedicated to working – I thought I had the job. I used to train and guide new employees on the credit card sales process, too. During those periods, I used to work for 18 hours a day without taking my weekly offs. Who wouldn't want such a Team Leader? And this thought set my hopes high for the promotion.

Impossible Sales

Shortly after the interviews, the successful employee list was announced – my name was not on the list. I thought, maybe, the others were much better than me or had some excellent recommendations. In the next couple of days, I spent a lot of time trying to figure out what could have been the reason. Well, I didn't find any. My work was my passion, so I immersed myself in it, and my colleagues were very supportive. Two months later, we received another email from Human Resources. Can you guess what it was about? Yes, it was yet another IJP, and this time they wanted 10 Team Leaders. My joy knew no bounds as I declared to myself that this is it – I was going to become a Team Leader.

I prepared myself thoroughly for the interview, and as expected, it went very well. This time, I was doubly sure that I would be promoted, and I waited impatiently for the list. When they posted the list of the employees who were selected, I was shocked. I went through the list again to check whether I had missed seeing it or if it was an error by HR, but then reality dawned on me – I was not being promoted. To add salt to my wounds, I saw that the people, whom I had trained, had made it to the list, they were Team Leaders now. It was an extremely upsetting experience for me. My ego took a beating, my smile was replaced with anger, and my desire to work hard was replaced with thoughts of resignation.

The very next day, I entered the office with a resignation letter in my hand. Signed and sealed in an envelope. I felt strange walking in the office space, and I thought my colleagues were watching my every move. The new Team

Leaders were conducting team meetings and briefing their team members on their weekly and monthly goals. For me, it was probably the longest walk- a defiant walk of shame and anger. I decided to go to the HR department to hand over my resignation and walk out with my head held high. I told myself that this was my last day in the organization. On my way to the HR Department, I heard a noise coming from the cabin of the Training Director – Ronald James, a Canadian National working In Mumbai. He was the person who had trained us when we first started on this credit card project. I entered his cabin to share my final words before resigning.

He greeted me with a chirpy *"Wassup buddy"* probably unaware of my situation.

I replied, *"Ron, do you know what's in this envelope? It is my resignation letter. Today is my last day here."*

He did not react to my words. He calmly said, *"Did you forget the way? The HR department is on the 6th Floor!"*

So much for the sarcasm! This was the least expected reply, and I felt that this was indeed the end of the rope. With a dry smile and moist eyes, I turned around to open the door, and that's when I heard him say *"Mihir, I have a question for you."*

These words sounded sweet to me as I thought that finally, someone wants to know the reason for my decision. I turned around and said, *"Yes, Ron."*

Ron: *"You live in Borivali and travel to Powai, am I right?"*

I: *"Yes"* (surprised at the question)

Impossible Sales

Ron: *"That means you must be commuting via the Aarey Road?"*

I: *"Yes."* (Still trying to figure out why such a question)

Ron: *"Have you seen the construction workers who are making the new tar road?"*

I: *"Yes."* (!! ??)

Ron: *"Have you seen the construction workers with the heavy hammer breaking the big rocks?"*

I: *"Yes. I have."* (Getting restless with the questions)

Ron: *"Last question – Does it happen that every single time the construction worker hits the hammer on the rock, the rock breaks?"*

I: …… (speechless)

I got the answer that I was looking for – my moment of achieving enlightenment. I realized that it is not every single time when the hammer hits the rock that the rock breaks, consistent efforts, one blow after another, breaks the big rock into pieces. No further words were exchanged.

I had walked into Ron's room angry and disappointed, and as I walked out of the room, I knew that this was probably one of the most significant learnings of my life. I felt like a new person altogether, enlightened. I tore the resignation letter and walked back to my cubicle with a smile on my face. I joined the team, which was now headed by a newly appointed team leader (I had trained him), and continued hammering the rock. A few months later, there was another IJP – not for a Team Leader position, but a Sales Trainer position. After a test, an interview, and a demo training session, I was amongst the three chosen ones to create a learning legacy in the same organization.

As a sales professional, many things need to be done. As we have seen in the situation above, doing something just once does not guarantee success. Repeated efforts bring you closer to your goal. There might also be times when you feel that things are not going as planned. And that might lead you to question your logic of continuing with your attempts.

You might even want to give up. But, remember, if the rock needs to be broken, consistent hammering is required. And if you feel that the efforts have been consistent without any positive signals, it might be just that the time has come to change your strategy. But the rock needs to be broken!

How Does Consistency Help?

As an example, we will see how it works with prospecting on LinkedIn, an online social network for businesses and professionals. Today, you have higher chances of attracting clients in the digital world by building your reputation and trust. This does not replace traditional methods of doing business but simply expands the horizon and helps organizations and individuals to be on par with others in the business environment.

LinkedIn is a networking site for professionals. So, it is always better to create your footprint there. Take steps to make you successful on LinkedIn.

[TIME FOR ACTION]

One Time Tasks:

1. Have a Corporate Headshot Picture as your profile picture (First impressions are the best ones)

2. Use a prominent yet Unique Headline which says what you are capable of

Recurring Tasks:

1. Use search parameters and connect with potential customers/decision-makers

2. Request for Testimonials (positive testimonials influence buying decisions)

3. Write posts which are related to the challenges and solutions faced by your potential customers

4. Upload photos (either with your colleagues or customers)

5. Attend events, seminars and conferences and upload photos taken there

6. Wish people on birthdays, congratulate on work anniversaries, and new jobs

7. Celebrate milestones digitally by posting updates or uploading photos (such as you getting awards, rewards, and appreciations)

Some More Action Points:

If you add a 100 contacts daily, that means you have 3000 contacts in just a month (and you will be celebrating three milestones – reaching 1000, 2000 and 3000 customers!).

Have a target of one 'issue-solution' post every month, and in a year, you would have shared twelve problem-solving solutions.

Sharing photos, on your profile, with your colleagues and customers convey that you are a friendly person, a team-player who gets along well with others.

Wishing people on birthdays and anniversaries creates engagement with your contacts, and they would be more receptive to your posts and updates. Please write a personalized message instead of a standard *Happy Birthday* or *Congratulations*.

Have an impressive signature, as this is your advertising opportunity.

Doing all of this might take 30-40 minutes a day, but it establishes you as a brand in the market. Seemingly small daily improvements will give you incredible, long-lasting results.

Implementing this in the non-digital world is time-consuming. The following activities are examples:

   a. Chalk out a communication frequency plan for existing and new customers
   b. Remember and wish people on occasions
   c. Send greeting cards
   d. Attend events and gatherings
   e. Hand out business cards
   f. Send emails related to industry updates
   g. Be well dressed always

One of the things that we must do consistently is to build a personal brand, a name that is both trustworthy and dependable. Always have a foot in the door, so that when there is a buying requirement, you are on the top of their mind.

Don't Eat The Marshmallow

Patience is another essential ingredient in the recipe for progress. People generally have an attitude of 'I want it now' because they lack the patience to let things happen at the right time. This approach is seen when they set goals and seek early gains.

Studies prove that delayed gratification is a crucial factor in the roadmap to success. Let us study the Marshmallow experiment to understand the benefits of patience. In the late 1960s, the American psychologist Walter Mischel carried out a series of experiments to study self-control and the role of delayed gratification in our life. He used the marshmallow test.

Walter and his team gave some selected preschoolers a plate of marshmallows. The children were left alone in the room with their treat (one or two children in a room) and were told that the team member had to leave the room for a few minutes.

The child was then a simple choice: The child could have two marshmallows if he or she waited till the team member got back or if waiting seemed impossible, then, they could ring a bell, and the team member would return immediately, but they would have just one marshmallow as a treat. Some of these children were able to exercise self-control instead of double the treat.

When the children became adolescents, the researchers carried out some followup studies. They found out that the preschoolers who waited for the second marshmallow (using their willpower to delay immediate gratification) had higher SAT scores. Their parents rated them on a higher scale when it came to planning, handling stress, displaying self-control in discouraging situations, and the ability to focus without getting distracted.

What Can We Learn From This Experiment?

The road to achievement has to be paved with discipline. It is easy to succumb to immediate gains, but in the long run, self-control, patience, persistence, and perseverance will ensure that success is your destiny.

How can we mobilize the power of waiting to achieve long-term goals in our life? Set small goals, commit to achieving them daily, keep track of your progress, and eventually, you will achieve your goal. Take baby steps.

As the saying goes, *"Don't make a permanent decision out of a temporary emotion."*

Rome was not built in a day. Each step you take today will bring you closer to your goal.

Take rational decisions when it comes to emotions and finances. Cooldown and think for a moment as this will help you in the long run. Successful salespeople know how to make use of the 'pause.' They assess the situation and then make their choices keeping their long-term goals in mind.

Be grateful for small victories, celebrate each one of them, love your journey, and not just the destination.

When you try the CIMTA approach of Sales, it is not going to be easy. You may not get it right initially. What matters is that you don't give up. Instead, focus on what went right and what didn't work. Tweak the approach and try again. Soon you will have mastered the art and will be making much more sales than earlier.

When you ask your team members to dig out the past data, categorize them, and form strategies, there will be reluctance, and this also requires consistency.

Initially, doing all the activities stated will disrupt your work-life balance, as you require time, effort, and energy to be invested. Take slow and gradual steps.

10 Celebrate Your Achievements

How to create more opportunities for celebration?

Celebrating Your Success

We learn from observing life. This statement brings to mind a visit that I made a few years ago to a friend's place. He was the proud parent of a one-year-old kid. The little boy was curious and wanted to know who I was, so I introduced myself and extended my arm and said, *"Shake Hands."* I remember teaching him the 'Handshake.' He had no idea what was expected as the action, and the words were new to him. He ignored it at first

> *"Happiness is not in the mere possession of money; it lies in the joy of achievement, in the thrill of creative effort."*
>
> – Franklin D. Roosevelt

then ran away, but his curiosity got the better of him, and he came back after a couple of minutes. When I extended my arm again and said *"Shake Hands,"* he looked at me and decided to touch my extended hand. I immediately shook his tiny hand, said, I smiled, started clapping and said *"Wow!"*

This child was surprised as he was not used to such appreciation before. I repeated the 'Shake Hands' activity, and the boy decided to extend his hand. I shook his hand, once again said *"Wow"* then smiled, and applauded him. He was amused and started looking around. I requested my friends to join the celebrations when we did it again, and the third time, he decided to give his hand on his own. I said, *"Shake Hands"* continued with the action, and said, *"Wow" and* clapped with my friends joining me in the celebrations. This was very exciting for the kid. Within 4 minutes, that little boy learned how to shake hands. His father tells me with pride that whenever he meets someone, he extends his arm and offers a handshake.

Kids learn because they delight in discovering new things. They focus their attention on what's important and ignore those that are meaningless to them. There is something very extraordinary in this ordinary phenomenon.

As children grow up, the Wows and Claps are replaced by chocolates and cookies. In their teens, it becomes pocket money or the freedom to go out alone or with friends. When they reach adulthood and start working, it could be an incentive or a promotion. The essence remains the same, being recognized for doing something acts as applause and is a motivator that pushes us to do more.

Celebration affects both your mind and body. That's dopamine at work, one of our body's neurotransmitters that sends signals from the body to the brain. It is a biochemical compound that has a range of functions, most of which are not fully understood.

Dopamine is crucial for both physical and mental well being, and it helps to regulate sleep, attention, memory, learning, concentration, and motor control. It is one of the critical factors that decide behavior, cognition, motivation, and reward. Whenever we are rewarded for any activity, dopamine is released in our brain. We, then, want to continue with the same task as we want to be rewarded, and as time passes, this release of dopamine can lead to learning. Researchers have discovered that our learning relates directly to how much dopamine we have in our brains.

When you achieve your goal and do not celebrate the accomplishment, you divest yourself from a vital feeling that boosts your success. Whatever we achieve in our life is determined by our state of mind. So a celebration reinforces positive feelings and prepares us to face any challenge or opportunity with renewed vigor. On the contrary, if you do not honor your accomplishments by celebrating them, you are telling yourself that your work does not hold any value. The lack of a celebration creates a vacuum that will deplete energy, focus, and performance over time.

Celebrating success on your own by writing in a journal, or going on a shopping spree with family can bolster mood. You can include our colleagues in our celebrations, as well. This has added benefits as the people in your organization recognize you, and it also helps in expanding your business circle. Your happiness is contagious, and people want to be a part of it. They are influenced by your success and think of adopting similar strategies at work, and that makes you are a winner. You have not only reached your goals, but you have also inspired others. Success attracts success.

When employees observe that their work holds immense value and benefits the company, they are driven to give their best performance and delight in going the extra mile. Celebrations recognize the milestones they have achieved in the course of their work. Positive employee engagement is the direct result of appreciation and recognition. Businesses must pursue the best and most effective methods of acknowledgment to harness employee productivity. Build a culture that encourages, acknowledges, and honors hard work. Recognize achievements promptly and make celebrations a way of doing business. This will lead to an increase in employee engagement, loyalty, motivation, and productivity. This can be done by throwing parties, giving gifts, incentives, or a pay raise, and the achievement can be published in the business newsletter and website.

What happens when you do something that people laud you for?

You feel:

- Sense of Euphoria
- Sense of Achievement
- Sense of Pride

- Valued
- Extremely Happy
- Energized
- Motivated

Selling is a constant challenge and keeps you on your toes most of the time. When you have achieved your targets or crossed a barrier, it is time to celebrate. A celebration reinforces your capability; it tells you that you have broken a barrier, you have overcome a hurdle, and that things are possible. It emphasizes good behaviors and good habits, which made you reach that goal.

There was a time in the history of the Olympic games when shooters from the USA dominated the event. The average scores of the shooters representing the US were very high when compared to the shooters from other countries. An analysis was conducted to identify the reason and experts observed that the secret lay in the way the shooters were trained and coached.

Typically, while training, it is understood that if the distance is 25 meters, then the shooters line up at that length. They practice holding the rifle, breathing, and keeping minimal body movements, and once they have trained hard, they get ready to press the trigger. When they miss the target, they try to find what made them err and rectify it – again and again.

The US shooters were trained to shoot at less than a meter, and when they got used to hitting the bullseye, the distance was increased gradually. They were still able to hit the target. This process was continued until they reached the Olympic target distance.

What is the difference in the training procedure? There is a lesson to be learned here. The USA team was taught to hit the target, and they did it with great success as their actions were positive. What about the others? They were trained on 'how not to miss the target,' so the focus lay elsewhere. Their methods defined their success or failure.

Celebrations develop a mindset for success. Remember, there is a science behind it, the one that we referred to before. The 'rush' (Dopamine – the neurotransmitter, happy chemical) that we feel when we know that we have hit the goal. So the more you celebrate success, the more content you become.

Finally, what can we do to bring about success? We need to appreciate and praise those tiny steps that we take towards our goal. Internal motivation keeps us going despite the obstacles that we might face, the ability to recognize and celebrate even small wins is what will propel us towards future success.

Set **S.M.A.R.T.E.S.T.** goals for yourself but don't set out to capture the big picture in the first instant. Write down small steps that will lead you to the big picture. Make sure you don't forget to gift yourself something that you love when you attain a small goal. What do you enjoy the most? Is it food, chocolate, a movie, a book, the latest phone or a dinner with the family, and treat yourself every time you distinguish yourself.

Don't stress yourself and try to live in the moment. Plan your day by giving yourself small goals that can be easily achieved. Do not put a strain on your mind by giving yourself inflexible deadlines. Stay relaxed and focused by always permitting yourself a buffer period to accomplish your goals. Make a note of your progress so that you know how close you are to your goal.

This helps to motivate and keeps yourself on track to achievement. Highlight all your accomplishments as they are the milestones on your road to victory and happiness. Be good to yourself.

Celebrating Customer's Success

Be there when they need a solution; be there to celebrate their success. That's how professional relationships succeed – by having a partnership approach.

With your clients, it is as essential to be there when they achieve any form of success. Mediocre salespeople are only tuned in to transactions, and their entire focus is getting business from the clients. They feel that if they satisfy the requirements, and customers are happy with the purchase, then everything is going well. There is a different level of partnership when you are also present to congratulate and celebrate their milestones. Nurturing relationships need extra efforts.

What can you celebrate?

- Company Formation Day/Foundation Day
- Anniversary (of professional relationship)

Celebrate Your Achievements

- Birthdays of Leadership Team
- Bagging a Contract or Deal
- Meeting Yearly Targets
- Expansion – In terms of Locations or Products
- Awards
- Certifications Achieved
- Festivals or Events
- Transaction Milestones (number of sales orders fulfilled by your company)
- _____ and many more!

Keep track of important dates and have a dashboard for your key accounts. Use Google Alert service to keep a track. Also, build relationships with people from different departments in Key Accounts.

> *"The more you praise and celebrate your life, the more there is in life to celebrate."*
>
> *– Oprah Winfrey*

Your presence, one excitement-filled call, one genuine message, one handwritten note has the power to strengthen the relationship. You don't always need expensive gifts to celebrate. Thoughtful and timely gestures are for more enriching.

Celebrate the customer and the relationship, and the economics will take care of itself.

The Last Word

And why this is just a beginning?

Imagine yourself as a youngster standing beside a bicycle for the first time. You are watching someone ride this two-wheeled vehicle in a straight line and wonder how the rider maintains balance without keeling over.

An experienced bicyclist guides you on how to do it. You learn that by holding the handlebars steady and pedaling the bicycle until it moves forward without tipping over. You should steer gently with the handlebars and turn the front wheel in the direction you want to go, and manipulate the vehicle to avoid pedestrians and other obstacles. If you stop pedaling or even slow down, the bicycle can become unstable, wobbly, and will start to fall. If you want to halt, you have to press the hand brakes gently and be prepared to lower a leg for stability as you come to a stop.

This knowledge is enough to learn the essentials of cycling; however, it doesn't mean you can ride a bicycle. What you need is practice, and there is no better way to do that than to start riding. You learn to coordinate your movements and discover how rapidly you have to rotate the pedals to keep the bicycle moving, and to redirect the handlebars gradually to turn a corner. Only with repetition do you find out how to slow down and stop without tipping over. Once you master riding, what you have learned will stay with you for the rest of your life. You may abandon the bicycle for an automobile, and years later, take it up for exercise and find that in moments you are rolling ahead, fully coordinated, your brain responds to what you had learned in your earlier cycling days. As you perfect your craft through practice, you look back and remember the joy of finally getting on a bicycle and riding to your destination, without giving a second thought to the technique that now comes naturally.

Similarly, success in sales depends upon a thorough knowledge of the selling process. Reading this book would increase your sales knowledge; however, it would need the implementation to see the results. Consistency is the key here. Selling requires a three-pronged approach: a passion for sales, inherent knowledge of all aspects of sales, and a clear plan to reach goals. It takes practice, persistence, and self-belief to perfect the art of selling. Once you master it, you will not think about any of the techniques, as it would have become second nature to you.

> *"Impossible is just a word; IM-Possible is a way of life!"*
>
> – Mihir Koltharkar

And once you have learned the art, test your limits and ride in the fast lane. Learn to take the sharp curves. Measure the performance, explore different terrains, and continuously strive for the impossible.

Everything Works, If You Make It Work!

So, go ahead and craft your story. Draw your customers into the story and create the future you desire.

Tell me about the ideas in this book that have made a difference in your personal and professional life.

If you would like to learn in-depth or want a customized approach, do connect with me by visiting *www.impossiblesales.com*

I will be delighted to hear from you.

www.ingramcontent.com/pod-product-compliance
Lightning Source LLC
Chambersburg PA
CBHW021409210526
45463CB00001B/285